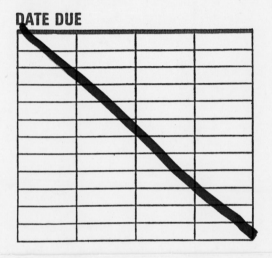

The Chinese Difference

The Chinese Difference

Difference

JOSEPH KRAFT

Saturday Review Press

NEW YORK

Published simultaneously in Canada by
Doubleday Canada Ltd., Toronto.

Library of Congress Catalog Card Number: 72–88660

ISBN 0–8415-0224-2

Saturday Review Press
380 Madison Avenue
New York, New York 10017

PRINTED IN THE UNITED STATES OF AMERICA

Design by Tere LoPrete

For Gil, His Brother's Keeper

Contents

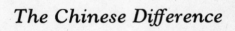

The Chinese Difference

I

☆

The Week That Changed the World

Toward the end of his China visit President Nixon met individually with each of us in the press party for a picture-taking session. He asked me, as we waited between shots, what I had been doing that day. I described a visit to the Soviet embassy in Peking for a reception and said the mood there was like the mood in Mudville after Casey had struck out. Mr. Nixon laughed, and I thought nothing more about it.

Until that evening at the end of a large, formal banquet given in the Great Hall of the People. The banquet broke up, as such affairs tend to do, in a semi-mob scene. Scores of people swarmed around the one exit from the Great Hall. The President and Premier Chou En-lai threaded their way through the crowd. As they moved, Mr. Nixon introduced Chou to various Americans, identifying us in an offhand way with what was plainly the first thought that popped into his head. A writer from a Chicago paper was presented as a man who came from a city as windy as Peking. A correspondent for *Life* was introduced as a fellow who wrote articles for a picture magazine. I was called a "Soviet expert." I supposed the reason for that inaccurate description was the encounter with the Preisdent earlier in the day. Again I thought nothing more about it.

Until about ten days later. By that time Mr. Nixon and his party had left China. So had all the journalists who came to China with the President—including a few who were allowed to stay behind for special interviews or to leave through Hong Kong. Whereas during the President's visit, when there were plenty of Americans on hand, the Chinese hosts showed little interest in the United States, I had become, as the surviving remnant so to speak, subject to almost daily grilling on current events by my interpreter or various officials in the Foreign Ministry. These sessions seemed to take place almost by accident, but they were inspired by some thought and covered a lot of ground. I was asked about the presidential primaries in the United States, about the Liberal Democratic party in Japan and the likely successor to then Premier Eisaku

Sato, about the comparative methods of the Associated Press and the United Press International, about the attitude of France toward the European Common Market, about credit terms for buying American aircraft, about the structure of the Christian Democratic party in West Germany and its implications for the security treaties with Russia and Poland. At one point, a question was put to me about the Soviet Union that I said I couldn't begin to answer. "But," my interlocutor, a young man from the Foreign Office, exclaimed, "the President told the prime minister you were a Soviet expert."

At that point, I formed my first strong personal impression of Communist China. High officials I had known previously in America and in other parts of the world had all been characterized by a fitfulness of interest. They hopped from subject to subject. If there was a single concern that engaged them for a long time, it was self. Their universal law was the McLandress Dimension (so-called by John Kenneth Galbraith after a mythical professor, Herschel McLandress), which purported to measure the length of time a celebrity could stick to a single subject without thinking of himself. The important, it seemed to me, had no sustained concentration, no capacity for paying attention to others. The world of the great was, above all things, Vanity Fair.

Not in China, however. Late at night, in the perfectly inconsequential setting of an exit from dinner, with scores of people jabbering incoherently of cabbages and kings, Chou En-lai had caught every word. Whatever else may be said about the Chinese, they have undoubted powers of concentration. They pay attention. They are different in deep ways, and this book is about the nature of the difference. It assays the difference in foreign policy and in the central domestic issue of the relation between agriculture and industry. It asks in particular the question of whether there has emerged in Communist China "a New Maoist Man."

My sense of the Chinese difference springs in part, no doubt, from secondhand experience—from pictures in the head that collect like stalactites bit by bit out of books and conversations and a thousand other experiences. I had been a Japanese translator during the war and had, then, conceived the impression that Americans tended to exaggerate enormously the importance and cohesion of China. That feeling was hardened by work done on the origins of the Open Door policy at the Institute for Advanced Study at Princeton in minor connection with what became George Kennan's first book, *American Diplomacy 1900–1950.* As a newspaperman working in Russia and India and the arc that runs from Japan south through Taiwan to Vietnam, I had been continuously aware of the Chinese shadow. Long before reaching China, I knew that it was an underdeveloped country, just past the stage of agricultural subsistence, still groping for a

path to industrial development. I knew too that it was
the theater of the longest unabated revolution in
world history—a continuing and deliberate turning of
the wheel that far outdistanced the celebrated revolu-
tions of France and Russia. I knew too that Thermidor, if it ever came, was still a long way off and that
the revolutionary fervor in some degree still gripped
the Chinese. It was not lost on me either that revolutionary infighting had raised a question respecting the
degree to which the center controlled the provinces;
nor that control over the provinces was open to only
two institutions—the Communist party and the army.
I knew too that China, as heir to an ancient civiliza-
tion, mixed revolutionary ardor with a cultural self-
confidence, which contrasted sharply with the social
insecurity—the positively arriviste mentality—of the
Russians. Not all of these preconceptions were radi-
cally altered by what I saw in China. But they were
hardened and reshaped, and in some cases utterly
changed. So let me first offer up the day-to-day itiner-
ary of what happened during the President's visit.

EN ROUTE TO PEKING: The President, in a statement
made as he leaves the White House, likens the China
trip to a moonshot. Even the few newsmen who play
cards on the way out do it differently. They play for
stakes designated in yuan, the Chinese currency. In
Hawaii, where we stop for a day and night, Mrs. Clare

Boothe Luce gives a dinner for some of the press and White House staff. Henry Kissinger is there and so is the President's secretary, Rose Mary Woods. Mrs. Luce's home overlooks the Pacific, but the truly staggering view is upstaged by her appearance—superbly dressed and with a black eye patch giving extra effect. She clearly wants to make the point that this is an hour when Henry Luce shouldst be living. She makes her point, like so many people, by couching it in an attack on liberals. "You liberals," she says, "don't really understand this trip. The important thing is its impact on the Chinese. Only the President can make that impact, and it will be a big impact because they know our record. They know that the British and the French and the Japanese carved out pieces of China. They know we Americans didn't. A hundred years ago their times of trouble and shame began. Now this is the end of that period, and it is symbolic that the Chinese pick an American leader to dramatize the change."

All of us, from the President on down, are reaching, trying to connect up the unknown with the familiar. In the process, there is already emerging a new American myth about China. It is the myth of China as a great power, able to shoulder some of the security burden borne for so long by the United States in the Pacific. It is a myth that is going to be very hard to down, for solid reasons cause Americans to itch for self-deception on China.

The central fact about relations between this country and China is that we are not much mixed up in each other's affairs. American security does not depend, in any clear and present way, on what happens on the mainland of Asia. Neither does American economic, cultural, or moral well-being. Precisely because we are not deeply engaged, China has been for American opinion a focus of narcissism, an occasion for striking self-adoring poses. The Chinese provide a stage for acting out, without having to pay for it, our own notions of American generosity and disinterest and concern for the underdog.

The Open Door policy was the first example of the myth-making bent. It rested on the implicit charge that the wicked Europeans and Japanese were illegitimately carving out for themselves hunks of Chinese territory. We Americans, in high-minded contrast, pledged outselves to maintain the "territorial integrity" of China. But from the turn of the century through 1950, no regime in China could even begin to assure law and order. The true choice for foreigners was either intervention or abandonment of all interests. That fact the United States recognized in practice by repeatedly winking at various incursions—particularly by the Japanese.

For our own self-esteem, however, we kept bright and burnished the legend of China's "territorial integrity." In the name of "territorial integrity" Washington took many of the steps that led to Pearl Harbor.

With the same thought in mind, this country, during the war years, heaped upon Chiang Kai-shek's China great-power attributes, including membership in the United Nations Security Council, which now seem absurd.

With the collapse of Chiang's regime, another myth was served up—the myth of aggressive Communist China, sponsor of subversive wars in Asia and Africa and the forcer of the revolutionary pace on the Soviet Union. Thanks to that notion, the United States didn't merely replace prostrate Japan as the balance against Soviet power in the Far East in the immediate postwar era. This country convinced itself it was helping peace-loving smaller nations stand up to the Chinese bully. Our presence in Southeast Asia was thus invested with the powerful moral purpose that worked to drive the United States so deep into Vietnam.

The new myth, while not easy to pin down, can be palpably felt in conversations with the White House staff and the press entourage accompanying the President to China. The immense achievements of the Chinese revolution seem to be accepted on faith. There is a strong disposition even to believe that there has been brought forward in China a New Maoist Man.

Between Mao's China and Nixon's America there are suddenly seen all kinds of harmonies. China is supposed to provide a way for the United States to get out of Vietnam. Big deals, especially in oil, are spied in the commercial field. Pressure from Peking is said to make Moscow more amenable to deal with Washington. There is talk—fueled by André Malraux, the French writer and romantic China-lover, who dined with President Nixon just before the trip—about a great future for economic aid to China. And the general assumption is, as *Newsweek* put it, that "China stands a good chance to attain the status of superpower."

In fact, the case for China as a great power is very doubtful. The recent disappearance of Marshal Lin Piao underlines the problem of the succession to Mao Tse-tung, which has already ripped China apart once. The role of the army continues to be in doubt. That puts into question to what degree Peking's writ runs in the provinces—how far, even now, China is a modern, unified state. Twice in the past, in 1941 and in 1965, distorted images of China have helped the United States talk itself into two avoidable wars. It would be a cruel mistake to go down that road again, no matter how pleasing to the self-esteem. So it is a sensible idea to be careful, very careful, about forming images of the new China.

SUNDAY: The Shanghai airport, where our press plane touches down in China around noon on Sunday, February 20, twenty-one hours before the President is due, looks like any other airport; its two-story rectangular terminal building, with a face of glass giving on concrete runways, could be in Cleveland. Before we leave the plane, a White House aide comes aboard to tell us that we are guests of the Chinese people, are lucky to be invited, and are in for a rare treat. As we come off the plane, we are greeted by a receiving line made up of a delegation from the Shanghai Municipal Revolutionary Committee. On the ground floor of the terminal, where we check our gear and pick up press credentials and cable cards, there are large pictures of Marx, Engels, Lenin, and—somewhat to my surprise —Stalin. A broad staircase covered in red carpet leads up to the second floor. At the top of the stairs, a huge portrait of Chairman Mao Tse-tung dominates the entire building. After climbing the stairs and browsing at souvenir counters, we are seated at tables for lunch. At each table is a prominent official of some Shanghai institution, who acts as host. The head man at my table is Wang Chin, a shrewd-looking man of about fifty, who wears a green cap and a green Mao jacket. Speaking through an interpreter, he bids us welcome and asks us about our trip. As we dig into our food, Mr. Wang tells us he is a newspaperman himself— an editor of a major Shanghai paper, the *Liberation Daily*. He says that, as a colleague, he will be glad to answer our questions and help us in any other way he can. He reminds us that in the old days Shanghai had been known, because of its wide-open, permissive atmosphere, as "the paradise of the East," but that now all the prostitutes, thieves, and drug addicts have been reformed. Industrial production has gone up fourteen times. We ask about the effect of the Cultural Revolution, and he says that since the end of that event, production has gone up 60 percent. One of us asks about two leaders of the Shanghai Revolutionary Committee, Chang Ch'un-ch'iao and Yao Wen-yuan, who had been known as extreme radicals in the Cultural Revolution, linked to the former defense minister and heir apparent to Mao Tse-tung, Marshal Lin Piao. Mr. Wang says that both men are busy in Peking. He denies prevalent rumors that Mr. Yao owes his meteoric rise to kinship with Mao Tse-tung and says such reports have been spread about by the Russians to discredit the People's Republic of China. With the talk flowing so easily, I decide to throw in a sensitive question. I ask what has become of Lin Piao. With total composure, Mr. Wang points toward the main dish in the center of the table and says, "Why don't you have some more mandarin fish?"

Peking, a couple of hours later, presents the same model receiving line. We are bundled into buses for a twenty-five-mile drive to our hotel, in the main part of town—on the same street as the huge Gate of Heavenly Peace, where the regime stages its big public celebrations. My first impression as we drive into Peking is of a mercantile and industrial town in the Midwest. The countryside is flat, the streets are straight and broad, and the place is landlocked. Factories abut government palaces, and next to the factories are orchards and dairy farms. Walking or cycling, the people on the street do not have what I think of as an urban rhythm. They move slowly—at a countryman's pace. Suffusing the whole atmosphere is the smell of soft coal.

Our hotel, called the Hotel of Nationalities, stands next to a large museum. First, we are all assembled in a wing of the museum that has been set aside as the pressroom, and an official from the Information Department of the Foreign Ministry gives us elaborate data on arrangements for filing cables and making phone calls. An interpreter has been assigned to approximately every two American reporters, and he is also to serve as a guide and general helper—watchman, too, it soon becomes clear. Stanley Karnow, of *The Washington Post*, and I have made prior arrangements to see a certain European ambassador on our first evening in town. We are told that no cars are available. Or taxis. Or buses. Somewhat panicky, we call up the ambassador, who sends a car and driver.

The ambassador is a square-jawed pedant with the looks and enunciation of a schoolteacher, which is what he used to be. Back in 1969, he played a role in setting in motion the events that led to the President's trip, which now interests him passionately. With some disapproval, he asks why the President has seen

André Malraux before leaving Washington. He expressed doubt about Malraux's prediction that Chairman Mao would ask the President for economic aid. Mao, he tells us, is interested not in the day-to-day management of affairs but only in broad philosophical questions. The ambassador moves on to the question of Vietnam. He tells us there has been intense traffic between Hanoi and Peking in the past few months: Prime Minister Pham Van Dong, of North Vietnam, has been in Peking; Vice-Premier Li Hsien-nien, of China, has been in Hanoi—and so, though there has been no announcement of the fact, has Premier Chou En-lai. He believes that relations between Chou En-lai and Pham Van Dong are very good. Pham Van Dong himself had said he would go to Paris to push the peace negotiations with the United States, but that possibility had been aborted by the President's speech of January 25, broaching a new American plan for Vietnam and detailing the history of Henry Kissinger's secret negotiations with Hanoi. The ambassador says that Chou En-lai will tell Nixon just what he has already told Kissinger: that there are two things the United States has to do, one being to withdraw all its troops from Vietnam, and the other to let a neutral government take over in Saigon. The ambassador believes that there is no push for unification of Vietnam right now, because North Vietnam can't bring it off and China doesn't want it.

MONDAY: Early in the morning, we go out to the Peking airport to watch the arrival ceremonies for the President. All sorts of advance indications point to a cool reception. Back in Washington, many of us were told by an intelligence official that the Chinese Party cadres had been alerted to view the meetings with the Americans through the optic of a directive written by Chairman Mao in August, 1945, on the peace negotiations then going on with Chiang Kai-shek. In that directive, Mao asserted that the Communist aim was to "gain the political initiative . . . win the sympathy of world opinion . . . and a state of peace," and stipulated that there would be only a small quid pro quo on the Communist side: "There are limits to . . . concessions." In the same vein, Chou En-lai had recently mused to a visiting British journalist, "Why shouldn't we negotiate with President Nixon? . . . For instance, in the past we talked with Chiang Kai-shek." Ron Ziegler, the White House press secretary, just before we left Hawaii for China, indicated that everything about the trip was up in the air—from the arrival reception to the question of whether there would be a final communiqué.

Despite these warnings, the stiff and cool formality of the reception is startling. In the most populous country in the world, only a few hundred people are there to meet the President of the United States. They include a score of officials, led by Premier Chou En-lai; members of his cabinet; an honor guard of army, navy, and air force men; and a band. No foreign diplomats have been invited. Ordinary people, even passersby, have been rigorously excluded—a sign of a dead-serious meeting, rather than the fun and games that would serve the President's political interests back home. Discouraging slogans, in white characters on red backgrounds, festoon the airport. One says, "Struggle, fail; struggle again, fail again; struggle until victory: that is the logic of the people." Another says, "Make trouble, fail; make trouble again, fail again; make trouble until doom: that is the logic of the imperialists and reactionaries."

Waiting restlessly in freezing weather, the journalists inevitably lapse into their favorite mode—wisecracking. "This is the best reception Nixon's had since he went to the AFL-CIO meeting," someone says. "When he sees this crowd," says another journalist, "Nixon will change his mind and come out for bussing." Just before the plane is due to land, a sententious Chinese official briefs us in English on where everybody is supposed to stand. The honor guard will be here, the band there, the receiving line in a third place, the lesser officials in a fourth place, the American press in a fifth place, other foreign correspondents somewhere else, and so on.

"What about the people?" William Buckley, of the *National Review*, asks. "Where will they be?"

"The what?" the Chinese official replies.

As it happens, the arrival ceremony comes off in fine

style. The American flag flies bravely beside the Chinese flag. The band plays "The Star-Spangled Banner" without mishap. The President, smiling, shakes hands with Chou En-lai. As they review the honor guard, Mr. Nixon makes nervous small talk. He mentions the length of the trip. He observes that Premier Chou has made many long trips. The premier is impassive. Visible evidence that all is not just dandy in *his* government is given by his entourage. The premier, who is himself seventy-three, is followed by two leaders of even greater age—Marshal Yeh Chien-ying and the writer Kuo Mo-jo, who must be well into his eighties. The toll taken by the leadership fight resulting from the Cultural Revolution is reflected by the number of acting and deputy ministers. There is no minister of defense, no minister of state security, and no Party leader from Peking. All have been recently purged.

The substantive talks were scheduled to begin this afternoon, but the first news is of delay. For unexplained reasons, the President does not show up at the Great Hall of the People, in Tienanmen Square, on time for his meeting with Chou En-lai. Crazy rumors begin to fly. One of the most far-out has it that the President, instead of meeting Chou on schedule, has been called to a session with Chairman Mao. Most of us agree that this is probably ridiculous. And then we learn that the President has indeed met with Chairman Mao. Although the session appears to be largely symbolic, it is the first time in recent years that the chairman has received any foreign statesman on the first day of a visit.

At the formal banquet in the evening, Chou En-lai seems to speak from the viewpoint of eternity, while Mr. Nixon expresses eagerness to get something in a hurry. Three times, he speaks of the pressures on the negotiators to come up with some agreement. As one reason for action, he points out that "at this very moment, through the wonder of telecommunications, more people are seeing and hearing what we say than on any other such occasion in the whole history of the world." Next, after referring to "my eldest daughter, whose birthday is today," he asks, "What legacy shall we leave our children?" Then he stresses the urgency yet again—in, of all things, a quotation from Chairman Mao: "'So many deeds cry out to be done, and always urgently. The world rolls on. Times passes. Ten thousand years are too long. Seize the day; seize the hour.'"

TUESDAY: In the morning, instead of seizing the hour, most of the American party, including the President and Mrs. Nixon, rest. As they take their ease, there arrives unmistakable evidence of Mao Tse-tung's extraordinary position in Chinese life. The chairman really is a living legend. His name draws the sword from the Chinese stone. He is the Great Helmsman by force of more than metaphor.

Until the President met with Chairman Mao yesterday afternoon, Mr. Nixon's visit received only minimal attention from the public and in the press and radio. But immediately after the meeting with Mao, the freeze goes off. The local radio begins reporting Mr. Nixon's every move. *Jenmin Jih Pao* (the *People's Daily*), the organ of the Communist party's Central Committee, carries a picture of Mr. Nixon on the front page and eight different stories on his first days' activities. Large numbers of people, in a development apparently unprecedented in Peking, line up to buy the paper.

Mao's interest in the Nixon trip is, of course, nothing new. Premier Chou En-lai constantly cited Mao's name when he mentioned the trip in the past. There is on record the invitation to Mr. Nixon, which Mao issued through the late Edgar Snow. What is new is the chairman's willingness to have his identification with the Nixon visit made known in the most public and dramatic way to the leadership and people of China. The unmistakable personal stamp of endorsement Mao has placed on the Nixon visit carries an important long-term implication.

The coming generation of Chinese leaders is a closed book. It has not, in the fashion of Chou En-lai and other present leaders, been reared on the classics of Chinese and Western thought. It has not ex-

perienced, as Mao has, bitter disappointment with the sour turn of developments in the Soviet Union. Thus it is possible that the younger leaders will take seriously China's pronounced anti-American rhetoric of the past—will, in fact, move their country into a position of abiding, and maybe even dangerous, hostility toward the United States.

By leaning the other way now, Chairman Mao mortgages the future. He imparts to the notion of getting on with the United States the most weighty possible endorsement. He starts a thick barrier against the future Chinese leaders taking it into their heads to turn toward Moscow in the one combination that could truly jeopardize American security.

Thus, Chairman Mao's action has not only shaped President Nixon's trip but has also opened a line for the future. It is now possible for the United States and China to develop in time a normal relationship. And that possibility, which no less a figure from the United States could have achieved, alone justifies the trip that has brought Mr. Nixon here to Peking.

I lunch with a group of diplomats from Canada and Great Britain, most of them China experts. They all agree that the President's meeting with Chairman Mao and the coverage in the *People's Daily* are extraordinary. They insist that the purpose of all this special attention is to line up the Party and the people of

China behind whatever results from the meetings with the Americans, but certainly there is no indication that China has gone soft on the United States.

After lunch, I visit a military attaché from a country that is supposed to have a particularly sensitive appreciation of Chinese internal politics. The attaché, a colonel, offers a theory about how internal Chinese politics has recently meshed with foreign policy, particularly in the case of the President's visit. According to his theory, the army—led by Marshal Lin Piao, with the backing of Chairman Mao and the cooperation of Premier Chou—emerged from the upheavals of the Cultural Revolution as the dominant institution in China. Chou utilized it as the chief instrument of administration, particularly in the provinces, and thus it was supreme over the government and the Party.

But while the army was gaining the foremost role internally, China suffered heavy setbacks in foreign policy. There had formed around China a hostile ring, beginning with Russia and extending through Japan and the American-backed forces in Taiwan and Southeast Asia to India. In August, 1970, at a plenary session of the Central Committee, Mao and Chou, according to the colonel, decided to call a halt to the army's supremacy. They began rebuilding the Party and the government. They met with resistance from Lin Piao, his radical allies, and some of the top military commanders. In the course of the fight, Mao and Chou began to seek support among the provincial chiefs and

the old marshals, many of whom had been attacked in the Cultural Revolution. As part of their assault on Lin Piao, Mao and Chou moved to break the ring around China. A dramatic gesture, they decided, would be to pick up an offer, made in the spring of 1971 by President Nixon, that he visit China. When the Nixon visit was announced in the summer of 1971, Lin and his followers made it a test of strength. Chou and Mao won a hotly contested victory sometime that September, and Lin was forced out of office, and perhaps even killed.

Some support for the colonel's theory comes on Tuesday night. At a cultural performance for the American party, the hostess is Mao's wife, who ordinarily uses her own name, Chiang Ch'ing. She was known as a radical figure in the Cultural Revolution, hostile to the bureaucracy of the Party and the government, and cordial to the leadership of Lin and his military comrades. According to one Cultural Revolution poster, she charged that the wife of Liu Shao-ch'i, a well-known Party leader, who was purged in the Cultural Revolution, had behaved in a way that was "frivolous and in bad taste for a revolutionary" while acting as hostess during the visit of a foreign dignitary. Though not frivolous or in bad taste, Chiang Ch'ing is, on Tuesday evening, not revolutionary, either. She wears a well-cut black wool suit and chats amiably with the President and Mrs. Nixon. Most of the American experts present are convinced that the one reason Chiang Ch'ing has come to the performance is that, as one of them puts it, "the old man made her."

The evening reflects a similar softening of attitude. As late as the time of the President's arrival in Peking, it was believed that the Chinese would put on, for the Nixons, a performance of *Shajiabang*, a revolutionary opera that ends with a Communist guerrilla raid against troops of the Japanese-run puppet government in the Second World War. The State Department had said of *Shajiabang*, in an internal memorandum, "This is a viciously anti-Japanese play, which would probably not be appropriate for viewing by the President and Mrs. Nixon." Instead, the Chinese put on *Red Detachment of Women*. It is a ballet drama, danced with many classical steps to modern music largely played by Western instruments, that tells the story of a young servant girl, Wu Ching-hua, who is driven to join the Communists because of the beatings of a cruel master known as the Tyrant of the South, a minion of Chiang Kai-shek's. Eventually, the girl leads a Communist attack that achieves a complete victory over the Tyrant, who is killed, along with the troops who are trying to protect him.

WEDNESDAY: We fan out on various tours arranged by our hosts. With three other journalists, I go to the Dongfang Hong ("the East is Red") automobile plant,

housed in a red brick building, on the outskirts of
Peking which looks as if it might have been a school.
We are taken through the plant, which is a factory for
assembling jeeps, by Ching Ping, the head of the
plant's revolutionary committee, a handsome man
with a wide smile and strong features, who had been
an army battalion commander, and his assistant, Fung
Ke, an intelligent-looking, angular-faced former
municipal official in Peking, who does most of the
talking. The basic facts are that the plant turns out
10,000 jeeps a year, each one costing about 11,000 yuan
(some $4,500 at the official rate for the yuan, which is
about $.42) in labor and material, and selling for about
14,000 yuan (about $6,000), with the state raking in the
profits. There are 8,000 workers in the plant, a third
of them women. They are on the job six days a week
and eight hours a day. (Days off are rotated. There is
no officially ordained day of rest in Communist
China.) Wages are determined on the basis of eight
different grades set up by the revolutionary committee
to measure skill and seniority. The average salary is 50
yuan per month; apprentices get 34 yuan per month;
and the highest-paid workers take home 108 yuan a
month. Mr. Ching draws 196 yuan a month, and Mr.
Fung receives 170. There are no bonuses. "In the past,
we used to have bonuses," Mr. Fung explained. "But
during the Cultural Revolution we learned that
bonuses were a revisionist device, and so we stopped
them."

The work pace seems relatively relaxed. Nobody is standing around idle, but neither is anyone moving very fast. On the walls are numerous injunctions to study the thoughts of Mao, and Mr. Ching indicates that, thanks to such study, production has recently been doubled, from 5,000 jeeps per year to 10,000. I try a couple of times to discover precisely how Mao's thoughts have helped to raise output. On one occasion when I pose the question, I am shown how front-end grilles are picked up by an overhead belt and dipped into a bath of paint. Formerly, it is explained, they were sprayed one by one. When I pose the question again, I am shown a West German machine for making wire. Giving up on that line of research, I ask Mr. Ching what impact the Cultural Revolution had on the plant. He says, "There was an ultraleft tendency in the factory. They claimed that our work rules, and even our safety regulations, were badges of bondage, and they did away with many of them. Production became chaotic and slumped. But now that is over. The good work rules and the good safety regulations have been restored."

A French friend takes me to lunch at a Szechwanese restaurant on Wang Fu Ching Street, the best-known shopping street in Peking. The place has two levels— a cafeteria on the ground floor and a proper restaurant, with waiters, one flight up. My friend tells me that restaurants are the only places where one can meet Chinese people in Peking, because there are no clubs or cafés. At this very spot, he says, he once met some of the leading dancers from *Red Detachment of Women*. The food is spicy and excellent, and the cost of the meal is about five yuan (two dollars) for both of us.

Afterward, my friend and I visit some of the nearby shops. One is a traditional pharmacy, where the chief product seems to be ground horns of deer, served up in dozens of different varieties as an aphrodisiac. At a secondhand store, a brisk trade is going on in old mandarin coats—sheepskin on the inside, blue cloth outside, decorated with slogans or proverbs in lovely gold lettering. We end up at a modern bookstore. There are some young men buying the works of Mao, Lenin, and Marx, which are sold at one counter, but far more buyers are standing around a counter that displays criticism and history, where two works—a study of Tang dynasty poetry and a modern history— have just gone on sale for the first time since the Cultural Revolution. They are moving fast.

The evening program for us Americans is a sports spectacle—acrobatics, Ping-Pong, and so on—and I decide to skip some of this and drop in at the reception honoring Soviet Armed Forces Day at the Soviet embassy, to which a Russian diplomat I have met on an earlier occasion has offered to escort me. A sadder party there never was. My Russian-diplomat friend points out as we enter that the Chinese have changed the name of the street on which the Soviet embassy stands from West Legation Street to Antirevisionism Road. Only a very few Chinese are on hand, most of them standing in small groups in the far corners of a room that is the size of a football field. The Russians themselves are full of nasty cracks about the Chinese and elaborate suspicions of President Nixon's trip. One Russian points out to me that whereas the Chinese have called Mr. Nixon's visit with Chairman Mao "frank and serious," they called a meeting not long ago between Aleksei Kosygin and Chou En-lai just "frank." Another Russian tells me that the Chinese have forgotten how to speak Russian. A North Vietnamese diplomat is on hand, but when I approach him he tells a Russian who starts to introduce us that he does not want to shake hands with an American. At length, I meet the Soviet ambassador, Vasily S. Tolstikov, the former Party boss in Leningrad, who is supposed to have lost out in the leadership struggle that brought Kosygin and Brezhnev to the top in 1964. Tolstikov looks the part of an apparatchik. He has a huge head on a short, powerful body. He speaks sparingly. When I tell him I think President Nixon hopes that his visit to Peking will help improve the climate for his Moscow visit, scheduled for May, Tolstikov stares at me in utter incredulity. "We'll have to see about that," he says.

THURSDAY: Everybody is up early for what is supposed

to be the sightseeing high-point of the trip—the Great Wall of China. After a forty-mile bus ride, hardly any of us has anything to say about the wall, least of all the President. He walks up and down, self-consciously shaking hands with a few Chinese, who seem to have been strategically placed for the television cameras. He introduces Barbara Walters, of the *Today* show, to Vice-Premier Li and tells him about the TV coverage of the sports exhibit the night before. He expresses disbelief and wonder at the building of the wall: "Imagine climbing all these mountains carrying stones." On the way back to Peking, we stop off to see the famous tombs of the Ming emperors. Once again, there is the problem of what to say. Mr. Nixon says, "When one sees these tombs, while this does not go back very far in China's history—its history goes back thousands of years rather than hundreds—it is again, of course, a reminder that they are very proud in terms of cultural development and the rest, a rich history of the Chinese people. As I said earlier, it is worth coming sixteen thousand miles to see the wall, and it is worth coming that far to see this, too."

Perhaps because he is bored stiff, Mr. Nixon, for the first time during the trip, suddenly seems eager for questions from the press. He is asked whether he would recommend that Americans apply for tourist visas to China. He replies, "I think it would be very valuable and worthwhile for Americans—and, for that matter, people in all countries—to be able to visit

China." Given the toal absence of news about the official talks, that comment looks like a hot item. Practically everybody assumes there has been agreement on exchanges of some kind in the cultural and scientific and touristic fields, at least. Suddenly speculation begins to center on what will be in the final communiqué.

FRIDAY: Mr. Nixon imparts a powerful thrust to the speculation while we tour the old Imperial Palace, known as the Forbidden City. The Forbidden City symbolizes, even more than the Great Wall does, the inward-looking nature of Chinese life and history. It is a series of ornately decorated palaces and courtyards, one leading into the next, until finally one reaches the sanctum—the private rooms of the old emperors. Snow has fallen in the night, and the exterior setting is beautiful. But moving from hall to hall at a breakneck clip soon becomes tedious. Stopping in the Hall of Supreme Harmony, Mrs. Nixon tells us she has spoken that morning to her daughter Julie, in California, and that Julie has reported that the color television of the visit is beautiful.

Our guide, the elderly Marshal Yeh Chien-ying, is himself less than ecstatic. Standing in one of the imperial bedrooms, he says, "They didn't pay much attention to their health when they slept here. The air

was not fresh at all." Later, he remarks, "If it were not
for the visit of the President, the people here would
seldom think of coming to visit the Forbidden City.
We do not have time for it."

Now Mr. Nixon has relaxed perceptibly, and he
begins introducing various press people to Marshal
Yeh. He introduces Courtney R. Sheldon, of *The Christian Science Monitor,* and when Marshal Yeh says he
knows of the paper Mr. Nixon reports that Chairman
Mao has said he, too, reads the *Monitor.* The President
introduces William Buckley with the remark "Buckley is very liberal—sometimes."

At the end of the tour, after a stop in the palace
museum, joy is unconfined. A reporter asks Mr.
Nixon how the visit is going. He says he'll have something to say about that in his toast at the dinner tonight. Marshall Yeh says, "It is my hope that people
of our two countries and people of the world can enjoy
peace and good harmony."

That sanguine comment sends expectations soaring.
By banquet time in the evening, it is universally believed that Mr. Nixon has achieved a spectacular
breakthrough. "He's got a blockbuster," someone says
in the press bus on the way to the banquet.

The blockbuster turns out to be a dud. Mr. Nixon
seems preoccupied at dinner. He builds his toast
around the visit to the Great Wall. He calls it "a reminder that for almost a generation there has been a
wall between the People's Republic of China and the

United States of America." He says, "In these past four days, we have begun the long process of removing that wall between us." Except for a cryptic remark that "the general trend of the world is definitely toward light and not darkness," Premier Chou En-lai offers nothing in his toast that points toward agreement, either. The two men leave the Great Hall of the People walking side by side but not speaking. As they go downstairs, Mr. Nixon suddenly sees the TV cameras. He begins moving his lips as though in conversation, but if he is saying anything it does not engage the interpreter.

In the pressroom tonight, the talk is of "deadlock" and "failure." Ron Ziegler moves among the typewriters counseling caution and pointing out that the meetings are not over. He enjoys no great success. "I don't know anything about China but I know a lot about Ziegler," one White House correspondent says. "When he knows something I don't know, he shows it—there's a glint in his eye. There's no glint in his eye now. He doesn't know anything. What we see is what is. It's a deadlock."

SATURDAY: Last night was the long night of the China trip. Henry Kissinger and Ch'iao Kuan-hua, the vice-minister of foreign affairs, who headed the Chinese delegation to the United Nations General Assembly in the fall of 1971, worked until the early morning hours blocking out the general elements of a joint communiqué. As they worked, they cleared points with the President and Premier Chou. Mr. Nixon did not go to bed until 5:00 A.M. Discussion continued this morning, beginning at 9:00 at the Peking airport, where delegations from the American and Chinese sides have met in a plenary session. There is more talk between Chinese and Americans on the flight from Peking to our next sight-seeing stop, Hangchow, aboard a Russian-made Ilyushin-18. During the flight, Secretary of State William Rogers, who has been meeting with his opposite number, Foreign Minister Chi P'eng-fei, enters the talks with the President, Chou En-lai, and Henry Kissinger. At one point, the President moves from the conference table in the plane to a forward compartment, where he begins writing on one of the yellow legal pads he favors. A couple of hours after the landing in Hangchow, Ziegler assembles the press and announces that a communiqué will be released tomorrow.

Hangchow is a lovely lake city, renowned as a vacation retreat. Parks and gardens fringe the lakeshore, and there are classic views, some of which have been fixed in Chinese legend as the Ten Scenes. On Saturday afternoon, the official party visits, by boat, a scene known as Listening to Orioles among the Willows. Premier Chou and Mr. Nixon stop at a birdhouse called the Pigeon Pavilion and watch a couple of love-birds. The President observes to the premier that the scene "looks like a postcard with those mountains in the background." After the boat ride, the President invites all the members of the press to visit the guesthouse he is occupying by the lake. He poses for a group photograph outside and then for individual pictures inside. Standing outside, he speaks in impromptu fashion about the role of the press. It is bitter cold, and many of us cough and stomp our feet. Mr. Nixon seems to have lost his voice. Still he talks on. He says he understands our job and its difficulties. He speaks of "the A.M. cycle" and "the P.M. cycle" and the "the six-thirty news shows." He tells us he will write our publishers and ask that we get a raise. He says he knows that we like to have "hard news," and that not much has been available on the trip. He says the secrecy has been necessary because of the importance of developing relations between China and the United States. He says, "I had to put first the obligation of nurturing the relationship that is so delicate and that could have been jeopardized."

Though the President's little address is undoubtedly well meant, if offends many of the press people, who find its tone patronizing. Their reaction, however, appears to be lost on Mr. Nixon.

At the banquet tonight, the President is in fine fettle. He delivers his toast impromptu and expresses his appreciation of his interpreter. He reintroduces almost all of us to Chou En-lai. For me, it is the third introduction in four nights. Premier Chou also seems in excellent spirits. The China watchers in the party offer a possible explanation: absent now from the revolutionary committee that runs Chekiang Province, of which Hangchow is the capital, are two high-ranking officers—one from the air force and one from the navy —who were known as radical supporters of Lin Piao.

SUNDAY: This is Communiqué Day in Shanghai. After Peking and Hangchow, it is a joy to be back in what most of us consider a *real* city. Noisy crowds throng the sidewalks and bicycles fill the streets near the magnificent waterfront. A touch of lipstick and rouge, plus an occasional bright blouse or kerchief, make the women stand out. There are specialty shops for clothing, cutlery, bicycles, electrical and photographic equipment, toys, wine and liquor, bedding, and food. At the number-one Shanghai department store, which looks like Macy's, I check some prices. Hot-water bottles are four yuan; blankets are thirty-two yuan; a bicycle is a hundred yuan; a long-playing record of the music for *Red Detachment of Women* costs nine yuan; a couple of lipsticks are two and a half yuan.

Coming out of the store, I run into Henry Hartzenbusch, an Associated Press man, who was born in Shanghai, where his father was a General Motors representative. He suggests that we visit the house where his family lived. It is a two-story stucco affair in what used to be the French Quarter. Some of the windows are broken, the garden is untended, and it is obviously run-down. An old woman who seems to be kind of a block boss tells us that six families now occupy the house. She refuses to let us in, and she discourages a young man who seems ready to show us about. Another young man—a teen-ager whom we encounter in the garden—is bolder. He takes us into what used to be the dining room. It contains two large beds, a square table, a bicycle, a bookstand, a violin case, a flute, and a music stand. The young man tells us he lives in the room with his mother, a retired doctor, and his father, an employee of the municipal utility. He himself is in middle school studying chemistry. The books on hand include chemistry texts in Chinese and in Russian. The young man, who is also musical, tells us he plays both the flute and the violin. I ask him what he wants to be when he grows up. He replies, "I want to build Socialism and Communism in China."

At five-thirty in the afternoon, the communiqué is released, at a kind of theater adjoining the hotel where the press has been put up for the night. Henry Kissinger is on hand to answer questions, and so is Marshall Green, the assistant secretary of state for East Asian and Pacific Affairs, who is due to begin a tour of Asia the next day in order to pass on word about the President's visit to allied governments. The salient passage of the communiqué affirms "the ultimate objective of the withdrawal of all U.S. forces and military installations from Taiwan." In return, the Chinese promise steps to improve relations in the fields of culture and trade, and there is envisaged "the sending of a senior U.S. representative to Peking from time to time for concrete consultations to further the normalization of relations between the two countries."

At the final banquet, Sunday night, Chou En-lai, expansive and chatty, keeps knocking back glasses of the Chinese firewater, *mao tai.* Some of the younger radicals, however, are still shrinking from contact with the United States, it seems. Chang Ch'un-ch'iao, the head of the Shanghai Revolutionary Committee, says of the President's visit in his toast that "we people of Shanghai . . . welcome this positive action," but he emphasizes the point that "in the twenty-three years since the liberation of the city in 1949, fundamental changes have taken place," His chief associate, Yao Wen-yuan—the ideologue of the Cultural Revolution, who is said to be related to Chairman Mao—does not show up for the ceremony.

On the American side, Henry Kissinger makes only modest claims for the meetings. At his briefing on Sunday night, he looks tired, and speaks not of immediate results but of "an attempt by two countries . . . to mitigate the consequences of . . . disagreements." President Nixon seems to have no reservations. In his final toast, he says, "This was the week that changed the world."

A self-glorifying, boastful bit of rhetoric that seemed to us at the time. At first glance, what had happened was that the Chinese Communist regime had suffered Mr. Nixon to use their country as a backdrop for a full week of glorious television played back in the United States at the outset of an election year. On the sixth day the Chinese had presented the bill. Mr. Nixon had balked—hence the surprisingly unfriendly tone of the dinner Friday night and the long sessions that lasted until dawn and beyond on Saturday. Despite his displeasure, the Chinese had plainly not given way, and in the end the President had had to pay their price. He had recognized there is only one China and committed the United States, at some date, to abandon support for the regime in Taiwan.

But that conventional judgment, which was my own at the time, did not reckon how the Chinese would turn the visit against Soviet interests. Neither did it figure how the Russians would rebound; nor what Mr. Nixon could make of their riposte.

After seeing the President off in Shanghai at the end of the visit, Chou En-lai came back to a hero's welcome in Peking. Madame Mao Tse-tung showed up as surrogate for her husband in an unprecedented airport appearance. Yao Wen-yuan, the radical director of propaganda for the regime, who did not surface once during the Nixon visit, was also on hand, an evident acknowledgment that not even the extreme Cultural Revolutionary Left could find fault in the way Chou handled the President. So warm was the reception, so pronounced the emphasis on the prime minister's name in the newspaper, radio, and television accounts, that some diplomats began to speculate about the making of a Chou En-lai cult.

With home base secure, the prime minister lost no time in turning to account against the Russians the assets accumulated during the Nixon visit. On March 3 he flew to Hanoi for meetings (not formally announced presumably because the North Vietnamese have never publicly mentioned the Nixon trip to China) with Prime Minister Pham Van Dong and Prince Norodom Sihanouk, the Cambodian ruler who was deposed in the coup of March, 1970. On March 5, after Chou had flown back to Peking, Hanoi released a communiqué summarizing the talks with Prince Sihanouk in terms highly favorable to China and prejudicial to the Soviet Union. The Chinese, who would probably like to see Indochina split among the states of Vietnam, Cambodia, and Laos after the war, have been pushing Sihanouk's claims to be the rightful ruler of Cambodia ever since the 1970 coup. The Russians, who maintain relations with the existing Cambodian regime, have been urging the North Vietnamese to squeeze Sihanouk out, the better for Hanoi to become the dominant power throughout Indochina. The communiqué asserted as never before a partnership between Sihanouk and the North Vietnamese. It spoke of "unshakable solidarity" and a "brotherhood-in-arms" that would run as long and true as "the majestic Mekong." It also cocked a snoot at the Russians. In a denunciation of outside meddling, Sihanouk and the North Vietnamese said, "The two parties declare that the problems existing between the two countries will be settled by the two peoples through negotiations in fraternal friendship without any foreign interference."

For a couple of weeks, it was not clear what Chou had given the North Vietnamese in return for their support of his Cambodian protégé and their slap at his Russian adversaries. But twenty-five days later, on March 30, the North Vietnamese kicked off in South Vietnam a vast offensive across the Demilitarized Zone and the Cambodian border. That event resolved all doubts about Chou and the North Vietnamese for at least one party—the Russians.

The Soviet Union had, of course, provided most of the wherewithal for the North Vietnamese offensive. For months the Russians had been sending planes, artillery, antiaircraft guns, and all kinds of other equipment by ship to Haiphong and other North Vietnamese ports. The heavy supply effort had been initiated in September, 1971—after the arrangements for President Nixon's Chinese visit had been made by Dr. Kissinger. Presumably, Moscow's response to the prospect of Sino-American cooperation was new support for North Vietnam. It was widely assumed that Russia wanted the North Vietnamese offensive to be timed as a kind of spoiler for the Nixon China visit. When, in fact, the timing turned the other way,

Moscow drew the reverse conclusion. The Russians assumed the Chinese had done to them what they had tried to do to the Chinese. Moscow figured Chou had given the green light for the offensive to spoil the visit Mr. Nixon was due to make on May 22. The Russians further calculated that if they let that happen, if the fighting in North Vietnam was able to bar the Moscow summit, they would leave the field to cooperation between Chinese and Americans for years to come.

Under those circumstances President Nixon was able to achieve an extraordinary diplomatic coup. He responded in a very tough fashion to the North Vietnamese offensive—mining the harbors and resuming the bombing of North Vietnamese supply lines and cities in a major escalation of the war. Rather than compromise the summit meeting with Mr. Nixon, the Russians took it lying down. Indeed, in the course of the Moscow summit they arranged to emphasize precisely those areas of Russian-American cooperation that the Chinese could not enter—arms control, incidents at sea, space and scientific exchanges. At the Moscow summit, the Chinese were the third party—a presence brought on the scene by Russian suspicions, but palpable in influencing every move. In the end it was not too much to say that the week in China had changed the world.

II

☆

The Chinese Miracle

Failure isn't supposed to breed success in American life. But that is not true of journalism, and a case in point is the story—still somewhat unclear to me—of how I happened to be the only American journalist to stay on in China for an extended visit after President Nixon's trip.

I had applied to go with the press party accompanying the President to China in the dual role of newspaper columnist and correspondent for *The New Yorker* magazine. The White House, much experienced in the gentle letdown, discreetly signaled to me, first, that no columnists would go, and, next, that *The New Yorker* would not be one of the magazines included on the press list. Somewhat miffed, I began pulling wires with the Chinese for a special visa independent of the President's trip. To my considerable surprise, a few days before the President's list was published, the Chinese came through. I was to collect a visa in Paris, be in China a week before Mr. Nixon's arrival, stay through his visit, and stay on afterward for an extra two weeks.

When the White House list was published, I found to my chagrin that I had been included. The Chinese, of course, immediately canceled the arrangements for a special visa. But when I reached China, I was able to argue with the relevant authorities that not to let me stay on now would be a kind of punishment—and thus unfair—for having been included on the Nixon press list. On the last day of the President's visit, an official from the Information Department of the Chinese Foreign Ministry told me that I would be allowed to remain behind. "We want you," he said, "to learn about our country."

In time I came to focus that mandate on the central issue of relations between agriculture and industry, life in the country and life in the towns. But at first, learning about China was like trying to understand a forest by looking at scattered pieces of bark. An excellent interpreter, Yao Wei, who had previously worked with Edgar Snow, had been assigned to me, and we began roaming around on what seemed to be an almost random basis. From Shanghai, after the President left, we flew to Nanking. Then we went by rail back to Shanghai. Then back to Peking. Everywhere there were curious, even baffling encounters.

In Nanking I visited a stupendous new bridge across the Yangtze. It is the Chinese equivalent of Egypt's Aswan Dam, a national showcase storied in film, song, dance, picture postcard, and visits by millions of ordinary citizens. But like many showcases, the Nanking bridge tells more than its promoters imagine. If it announces organized effort on the grand scale, it also speaks of weakness and division.

By any standards, to be sure, the bridge at Nanking is a supreme technical achievement. The river is nearly a mile wide at the point of crossing. It is, according to our guides, nearly 100 feet deep, and the bottom is so thick with alluvial deposits that the caissons had to be anchored far beneath the river bed. As the Yangtze is a major artery of commerce, vessels of 10,000 tons are eventually supposed to come up river far beyond this city. So to allow for such ships, the bridge has been built nearly 400 feet above the surface of the river.

All in all the structure runs about 3 miles in length, from approach to approach, and more than 500 feet in height from the caissons sunk below the Yangtze mud to the soaring mosaics of Red flags adorning the tops of the bridgeheads. It was built in eight years, from 1960 to 1968, which seems a short time. The more so as the Chinese built the bridge entirely by themselves. There were no Europeans to help as with the first bridge across the Yangtze at Chungking. Nor were there Russians as with the second bridge across the Yangtze at Wuhan.

On the contrary, our guide tells us how the Russians, having promised steel, "tore up the contracts" in 1960. He says that Chinese divers had to invent new equipment, and that one construction worker contributed so much that he was elected a member of the Communist party's Central Committee at its ninth congress, in 1969.

The official mimeographed description of the bridge stresses the theme of self-reliance even more. It says, "In accordance with Chairman Mao's teaching of 'maintaining independence and keeping the initiative in our own hands and relying on our own efforts,' China's working class designed and built the Nanking Yangtze River bridge with their own hands."

That proud claim is saved from vainglory by economic reality. The Yangtze divides North China, which is rich in industrial raw materials, from South China, which is rich in foodstuffs. Unlike the Pyramids or the Great Wall, the Nanking bridge serves a vital utilitarian purpose. Every day 100 trains cross the railway deck of the bridge. The top deck, a four-lane highway, is probably the busiest stretch of road I have

seen in China. Not for nothing does the official statement on the bridge quote a poem by Chairman Mao:

A bridge will fly to join the North and South;
A deep chasm becomes a thoroughfare.

But right there a negative point asserts itself. In a
country that is a continent with the largest populace
in the world, there are only three bridges crossing a
chasm that runs right across its center. Other lines of
communication—to the provinces of the far west, for
example, and within the mountainous regions—are
far more tenuous. Thus, despite enormous progress,
China is still not a cohesive whole.

In talking about the bridge, moreover, our guides
tell us of bitter disputes that attended the construction. One had to do with the width of the top roadway.
A second concerned whether the approaches should
be elevated on arches, as they are, or built on land
raised through grading. A third centered on whether
to put the Red flag mosaics atop the bridge towers.
These battles were fought in dead earnest and involved national leadership figures. During the height
of the Cultural Revolution, in 1967, construction was
stopped for a full month while debate raged. According to our guides, a minister of transportation was
dropped because of the stand he took on the width of
the top roadway. They also claim that Liu Shao-ch'i,
who was number-two man in China before the Cul-

tural Revolution, was involved in the fight over the flag mosiacs.

I cannot, of course, sort out these struggles. I cannot even tell the white hats from the black hats. But that disputes on such limited issues should generate such heat and rise to such leadership levels argues that in China evolution toward a stable political system still has a long, long way to run.

Having seen so much engineering, I thought I was entitled to a touch of culture. I asked to see some writers, and the authorities in Nanking served up two novelists and a poet.

Sun Yat-tien, the poet, is a thirty-six-year-old former electrical engineer with a rough face and hair worn crew-cut style. He worked for years in the coal mines and began writing verse on the side before he became a full-time poet. His regular income, paid by the writers' section of the local Communist party bureau, is about $40 per month, which compares with an average of $25 monthly for industrial workers.

Mr. Sun has published six collections of poems and one book of short stories. He recited one of his poems, which is translated as follows:

Red flags are flying at the mines;
They were hoisted in the year of liberation;
The backs of the miners have been straight ever since.

Ma Chun-yung is a forty-eight-year-old novelist, who draws about $70 a month in regular stipend from the writers' section. He has spent most of his life in the countryside and writes on rural themes. One of his novels, called *In Wind and Rain*, sold 30,000 copies.

Teng Feng-chang is a forty-two-year-old former newspaperman. Finding it "difficult to describe the deeds and high ideals of the workers in journalism," he started to write novels and short stories. He makes about $45 a month in regular stipend. One of his novels, which sold over 200,000 copies, earned him royalties of about $8,000.

The novel tells the story of a girl silk weaver who sets all the production records in her province. A new kind of silk is introduced in another province, and the girl is asked to weave it. Her family and friends warn against the switch, saying she will be less proficient with the new silk and lose her reputation. She decides to try the new silk anyway. In the end she sets a new record for production.

None of the three writers has had any books published since the Cultural Revolution began back in 1965. They hope they will be published in the near future.

In the meantime, according to Mr. Teng, "We have spent a lot of time going down to mines and communes and factories so we can get a good feel of the people. Our work needs to be rewritten and polished. We have to do a better job of presenting the heroes and heroines."

In particular, he feels, there is a need to emulate the eight revolutionary operas produced by Madame Mao, or Chiang Ch'ing, which tell dramatic stories of the victory won by the Communists over the Japanese and the forces of Chiang Kai-shek.

Under questioning, Mr. Ma, the rural novelist, offers an example of how living among peasants has enabled him to improve his own work. The first sentence of his novel *In Wind and Rain* begins: "We peasants are most afraid of typhoons and rainstorms in the autumn."

In the country, however, he met a peasant who told him, "I have read your novel. It's a good novel. But the first sentence is not true. It is true that there are natural disasters such as typhoons and rainstorms. But we peasants are not afraid of them."

I ask them about foreign authors. They have heard of Jack London, Mark Twain, Walt Whitman, Chekhov, Pushkin, Gorki, Tolstoi and Hemingway. I ask them how they compare the characters in Dostoevski and Chekhov, who seem to me so rich, with the characters in the revolutionary operas, which seem to me so flat. Mr. Teng answers.

Of Dostoevski, he says, "He is a very good writer, a very good depictor of character. But many of Dostoevski's characters are what we would call surplus people."

Of Chekhov, he says, "He gave a very good description of ordinary people. But he did not depict workers, peasants, and soldiers."

I ask what they think of Aleksandr Solzhenitsyn, whom I identify as the Russian who won the Nobel Prize in literature in 1970. Mr. Teng says, "During the time of Lenin and Stalin there were good Soviet writers. Now Russian literature has degenerated into revisionism. We are not interested in their work. I am sorry to tell you I have never heard of him."

They ask me about leading American novelists of the present time. I mention Norman Mailer, John Updike, Saul Bellow, J. D. Salinger, and William Styron. Mr. Teng says, "I never heard of any of them. For twenty years our relations have been severed, and we know very little about your country, but we are sure there will be more contact in the future because the people of America are a great people."

In making arrangements to see the writers, I had my first brush with low-level Party officials—a thirty-six-year-old Chinese apparatchik named Tao Yung-sheng, whose life story seems to explain what is probably the most striking feature of the Communist take-over of this country. That is the sheer staying power of the Chinese revolution, its enduring refusal to settle back to normalcy.

Mr. Tao is a member of the group set up to deal with foreign visitors by the provincial revolutionary committee that runs the province of Kiangsu, where Nanking is located. He attracted my attention because he was quick and intelligent and had something he pretended not to have—a working knowledge of English.

When I asked him his life story, he poured it out. He was born in Anhwei Province in 1935, to a family of poor peasants. The family came to Nanking in 1937, begging their way, Tao says, in search of more food. His father found a part-time job as a grounds keeper at the Sun Yat-sen memorial shrine.

For the next seven years the family lived from hand to mouth. Four of Tao's brothers and sisters died of starvation. He himself worked as a cowherd, a beggar in the streets, and as a tea vendor outside the Sun Yat-sen shrine. "I still remember," he says, "being slapped across the face by one of Chiang Kai-shek's men. He was an air force officer. He stopped for some tea. When I asked for money, he slapped me in the face. I will never forget it."

Tao will also never forget April 23, 1949, the day the Communists took Nanking. The next week he began going to school on a regular basis for the first time. He graduated from the Chinese equivalent of high school in 1957 at the age of twenty-one. His first job was as a teacher. While in that post, he taught himself English and met another teacher, a girl who became his wife.

"In the old feudal days," he says, speaking of the period before 1949 as though it were ten thousand years off, "marriages used to be arranged by the family. But I chose my wife."

The Cultural Revolution meant another step up for Tao. He was promoted from schoolteacher to his present job. He and his wife, who still teaches school, now make a combined income of about $45 per month. They and their two boys live in a two-room flat with 120 square feet of space. Every month they pay roughly $8.00 for food, $2.00 for rent, $1.75 for heat, $.65 for electricity, and $.06 for water. They rent their furniture from the state for less than $1.00 per month. They own wristwatches and a radio and have two bicycles.

Despite this relative comfort, Tao has no thought of taking his ease. He spends hours every week studying the works of Chairman Mao. He spent two months doing agricultural labor in a commune last summer. He believes in the treachery of many of the displaced higher-ups in the Party, including the former boss of this province, Chiang Wei-ching, and the former number-two man in China, Liu Shao-ch'i. "They peddled the theory that the masses of the people were backward," he says. "They thought they were more important than we were and that we were only fit for carrying baggage."

Given those beliefs and that life story, Tao is not prepared to bring the revolution to a halt. His experience has taught him that struggle means gain and that more struggle means more gain. So if the Chinese revolution is losing its fervor, if the Thermidor is approaching, the trailing-off period is going to be very slow—perhaps as long and drawn-out as the buildup.

As Tao puts it, "I do not want to make money and lead a comfortable life. That is selfish. I have learned to serve the people body and soul. We poor people fully appreciate what Chairman Mao has done. We are always ready to stand up for Chairman Mao."

The view of an apparatchik in action made me particularly eager to visit one of the unique features of the Chinese Communist party—the camps known as May 7 schools (after a relevant statement made on that date by Mao Tse-tung), where Communist party officials who stray from the straight and narrow go for discipline and reform. After considerable negotiations, I was able to visit a May 7 school about fifteen miles north of Peking. It houses some fifteen hundred persons, all of them from the West District of the city. They live in dormitories, ten to a room, get what seems to be ample food, and divide their time between studying the works of Mao and doing manual labor. The great bulk of the work involves clearing wasteland and raising rice. In addition there is the upkeep of the school, building dormitories, patching clothes, preparing food, and cleaning up.

Regular salaries are paid to those in the May 7 school, and every two weeks they have two days off. The majority own their own bicycles and pedal up to Peking; the rest take the bus. Theoretically a stint in a May 7 school is supposed to last six months. In fact about half of those in the May 7 school I visited have been there for two years or more.

Among those doing time there are some political types, clearly connected with Liu Shao-ch'i, the former Party leader whose fall from power was central to the Cultural Revolution. One of these is Ma Fenglin, a former Party secretary of the West District of Peking, whom I spoke to for about half an hour. Ma told me that he had joined the Party in 1941, served as a guerrilla leader during the civil war, and then became a security officer in the West District. In 1958, about the same time Liu Shao-ch'i was moving to assert full control over China, Ma became a Party Secretary in the West District.

In response to questions about what he had done that justified rustification in a May 7 school, Ma said, "At the beginning I did not think much of the Cultural Revolution. I did not understand what it was all about. Later on people criticized me. They said I came from poor peasant stock, and as soon as I entered the big city, I became bureaucratic and acted like a lord."

In 1967, Ma was, as he put it, "brushed aside" as Party secretary. He came down to the May 7 school when it was opened in October, 1968. Despite this long stay, he looked healthy for his fifty-two years and even seemed quite jolly. He wore a wristwatch, which is not all that common in China, and smoked cigarettes through a plastic holder, which is very uncommon. He said he expected to get back to Party work soon—though not necessarily as a Party secretary.

A far different—and I think more representative—

case involves a woman in her late thirties who had worked in a neighborhood Party organization keeping track of local production. Her organization was, as they say in the May 7 school, "simplified" during the Cultural Revolution. Her job was eliminated as a result. She has been at the May 7 school for three years, awaiting reassignment to another post.

I asked about her family. She said that she had left behind in Peking two children, aged five and thirteen, and her husband. Her husband worked in a factory and the thirteen-year-old went to school. The five-year-old had been sent to live at a state nursery.

I asked her if she missed the children. She said, "At first I missed the five-year-old. But I have grown accustomed to the separation. I see the family every two weeks and I know that the officials in the nursery take especially good care of children whose mothers are in the May 7 schools."

I came away not knowing exactly what to think. I am sure, of course, that almost all other May 7 camps are more harsh and farther removed from the big towns. I sense that apart from their political purposes, the schools are used as dumping grounds for the cast-offs of a bureaucratic system that has been chopped and changed at a dizzying pace. Still, judging by what I saw and considering the past hardships of this country and the standards of Communist leaders in other countries, I cannot believe that the rulers of China are the murderous butchers the American right wing is pleased to imagine.

By the time I visited the May 7 camp I had become aware of at least one central fact of Chinese life. Measured against a past that goes to the bottom of time, China these days is a riot of food. In all the major cities I visited, the markets were full of meat and fish and fowl, grains and fruits and vegetables—even milk and honey. The poorest villages I saw had reserves of rice, corn, millet, and wheat, and I found many peasants who kept large jars of these grains by their beds. At least a few restaurants—particularly the one in the old Broadway Mansions Hotel, which now serves as a government hostel in Shanghai—offer elegant meals. The canteens in factories, universities, and the May 7 school that I visited served luncheons of meat and vegetables, rice, and soup at prices that did honor to Socialism. In a Shanghai machine-tool factory, where the average wage is about $25.00 per month, the cost of lunch is about $.06. An office worker in Nanking, who together with his working wife earns about $40.00 per month, told me that he lays out between $6.00 and $7.00 a month in food bills for a family of four. In one village store I priced smoked fish at about $.10 cents a can, tangerines at about $.25 a jar, honey at about $.15 a jar, pork at about $.20 a can, and fresh apples at about $.15 a pound. "Nowhere," a Yugoslav shipping agent who has done business around the world and all over this country said to me, "can you eat so much for so little."

The horn of plenty has been filled by a decade of bumper harvests. Still, the string of fat years depends more on the works of man than the acts of God. In the past, a cruel environment dominated the life of the Chinese peasant. The vast interior plain of North and Northeast China is a dusty tableland, bare of vegetation, swept by dry winds from Siberia in winter, and drenched by torrents of rain in brief summers. The great river systems of the country—the Yellow River system in North China, the Yangtze in Central China, and the Pearl in South China—plunge eastward to the Pacific from the highlands of central Asia, depositing in their middle and lower reaches tremendous burdens of silt. Besides giving the Yellow River its name, the alluvial mud in many places raised riverbeds above the level of the surrounding fields. There was thus made up a cycle of disaster—of drought and flood, of erosion and waterlogging, of famine and death—ancient to the point of being called natural. An estimated 10 million persons died from starvation in the terrible famine of 1878. As late as 1938, there were deaths by the million from famine and floods in China.

Not for nothing were the Chinese Communists called agrarian reformers. When they came to power, they addressed themselves to these natural disasters with a vengeance. Millions of soldiers and peasants were mobilized to build public works designed to irrigate dry lands and control floods. The Red Flag Canal, a ditch about 100 miles long, was dug in the lower reaches of the Yellow River around Chengchow to water several million acres of Honan Province. More than 100 miles of protecting dikes, not breached in the past two decades, were raised along the valley of the Yangtze. According to *Geography of China*, a government publication put out by the Foreign Languages Press in Peking in 1972, since 1949

> the people have built more than 1,000 large and medium-size reservoirs and tens of thousands of small ones up stream on the bigger rivers, accomplished extensive soil conservation work and built several hundred thousand kilometers of dykes in the middle and lower reaches, and constructed 100 drainage canals in the low-lying plains and coastal areas.

The living symbol of this Chinese miracle is Chen Yung-kuei, an uneducated peasant, orphaned under shattering circumstances at the age of ten, who is probably as famous as anybody in the country except Mao Tse-tung. I went to visit Chen at his home base of Tachai, a remote mountain village in Shansi Province, which has been held up by Chairman Mao as a model for all Chinese agriculture. Once on the spot, the chairman's choice needs no explanation. The surrounding countryside, a treeless waste of gullies and ravines, presents the aspect of the Dakota badlands at their most bad. Amidst this desolation the village of Tachai starts out as an oasis in the Gobi. Its 800 acres have been neatly arranged in U-shaped terraces held up by stone retaining walls. A canal provides for flood control, and a reservoir assures a steady supply of water. Stone houses, each with a bedroom and a kitchen, have replaced cave dwellings. There are three stores (a food shop, a dry-goods shop, and stationery store) and a school for the 400 villagers. About 300,000 fruit trees have been planted, mostly in the very recent past. While much of the terracing and the clearing of the fields is still done by hand, and while horses and donkeys are used for hauling rocks and plowing, the village has just acquired four new tractors and a jeep. The grain yield, I was told, has increased more than tenfold since 1949.

The story of this transformation is the story of Chen himself. He was born in the early twenties to a family of poor peasants who moved to Tachai from Shantung Province. In the hard years of the early 1930s, his mother and a brother and a sister were sold as serfs to a local landlord; his father then hung himself. From the age of eleven on, Chen worked as a cowherd and farm laborer. When the Japanese entered the area in 1937, he became a kind of guerrilla scout for the Communists. By the time of the Japanese defeat, he was the local Communist leader, and in 1955, after guiding the village through land reform and then collectivization, he began the task of physical transformation.

In 1957 and 1958, floods washed out the work he had initiated. In 1963, a full seven days and nights of rain destroyed the terraces and flooded the caves in which the villagers still lived. Chen insisted on starting up again, this time using stone to build houses and shaping the retaining walls for the terraces in the form of arcs rather than straight lines. When he refused aid tendered by the state, his story, reported in the local press, came to the attention of Mao Tse-tung. In 1964, Mao coined the phrase "In Agriculture, Learn From Tachai." That slogan has subsequently been proclaimed all across China in a pamphlet and a film, and in millions of posters and postcards. Chen has been received by Mao on the chairman's birthday and has been visited in his home by Premier Chou En-lai. During the Cultural Revolution, he was made a member of the Party's Central Committee and a vice-chairman of the revolutionary committee governing Shansi Province.

We had dinner together after I had toured the village and seen the film that tells its story. Chen is a short man with gross features, bronze skin, and a stubble of beard. He lives, as all the other Tachai people do, in a two-room house, which I visited while touring the village. The house is distinguished only by pictures of Chen with Mao, Chou, and various East European visitors, mainly, I think, from Albania. He reads with difficulty and, I was told, can barely write his own name. He sported the peasants' uniform—blue trousers and jacket and a white towel wound closely around the head—and smoked constantly, lighting each new cigarette by stuffing into it the glowing end of the last one, thus not wasting even the butts. He spoke easily in the tones of a born leader, with almost no trace of jargon or affectation.

I asked him first about a recent editorial on spring planting from the *People's Daily*. He had seen it and had it broadcast to the whole village on its loudspeaker system. "It is very timely. Planting is the most important time for us. We have to make decisions then about how much land we can till, how much fertilizer we need and seed. Everybody has to come out to help. Even the children take a thirty-day vacation from school."

Though we were still on a first course of cold cuts, Chen at that point proposed a toast—to the solution of China's future problems. I asked him what problems he foresaw. He said, "Our main problem is that we don't have enough people in the village. Before the Cultural Revolution there was more labor than we needed. Now there is not enough. Why? The answer is very simple. Everywhere we are expanding agricultural production. So we need more hands to clear the land, and transport the grain, and do the sowing."

I asked him how he felt about *hsia fang*, a movement, much talked about by Chairman Mao, for sending young people from the city to work in the country. He said, "*Hsia fang* is no answer. Except for a few days at a time we have never had people from the city working in Tachai. Even those that came here were only from local towns, and they went home quickly. The trouble is that our country is so big. If you scattered the whole city population everywhere in the country, even that wouldn't make much difference."

I said that if there was a shortage of people in the villages and the movement from the cities couldn't solve it, agriculture was in a bad bind. He said, "Yes. The only way out is to go in for mechanization. We need fertilizers. We don't have enough tractors. We do not have enough motor vehicles. But to get those we need to increase production—especially the production of steel. Increasing steel production is now the highest priority."

I observed that Liu Shao-ch'i, the one-time chairman of the People's Republic and heir apparent to Mao, who was broken in the Cultural Revolution, had been ousted in part because he wanted to emphasize heavy industry, especially steel. Was Chen saying that Liu Shao-ch'i had been a man ahead of his time?

By way of reply, Chen first cited a line—"one divides into two"—of supposed philosophic wisdom from Chairman Mao that I was to hear to my invariable annoyance over and over again. "Chairman Mao teaches," Chen said, "that one divides into two. That means that in every action there are two possibilities, two lines—a revisionist line leading back toward capitalism and a revolutionary line leading toward Communism. The revisionist line is interested in making money. Liu was a revisionist. He was for anything he could sell. That's why he wanted to make steel. But he did not want to build Socialism. So he sabotaged the Great Leap Forward and the Cultural Revolution. Of course, we made many mistakes. In the Great Leap Forward, counties began building steel mills even if they didn't have the coke and iron ore. That was a mistake. In the Cultural Revolution there was turbulence and production actually dropped. But we had to rid ourselves of the revisionists. Now they are gone and production is coming back very rapidly."

But if the man who planted was enthusiastic about production, the men of industry had obvious reservations, and I encountered them in factory after factory. One factory I visited was a phosphorous fertilizer plant in Nanking. The manager there made no bones about the plant being one of the oldest in China: it was started in 1934. He said flatly that production could be increased only with new machinery. He pointed out that there was no room to expand along the crowded banks of the Yangtze. He allowed me to watch half a dozen workers with two forklift trucks, standing idle instead of loading the fertilizer bags. He himself demonstrated the weakness of phosphorus as a fertilizer— namely its tendency to burn up the soil—by taking a handful of the raw stuff from a barrel and skimming it across the factory yard so that it started small fires in several places.

In Shanghai I visited a much more modern enterprise—the Number One Machine Tool Factory. Among other things, that factory makes machine tools —some of them produced under conditions of constant temperature and humidity—with a tolerance for error of less than 1/1000 of a millimeter. But my guides did not point with special pride to these machines. On the contrary, the pièce de résistance at the Number One Machine Tool Factory is a workers' university, set up during the Cultural Revolution, that provides a special three-year course in six subjects (mechanical drawing, hydraulics, electricity, advanced math, machine design, and English) for workers who have not yet been to the university.

An even more impressive factory is the Peking General Petrochemical plant, an oil refinery built in 1968 in the austere western hills about fifty miles from Peking. The refinery produces an annual average of 2.5 million tons of gasoline and diesel fuels, 50,000 tons of lubricants, 30,000 tons of rubber, and 110,000 tons of fiber. It has 13,000 workers, who are on the job in four shifts night and day. It has vast storage tanks that take oil from the Taching fields in Manchuria, a complex cracking plant, and all kinds of machinery for processing and fabricating. There is a small computer to adjust the cracking machinery to varieties in the flow and quality of the oil. There is even a plant for purification of the waste water.

The head of the revolutionary committee that runs the plant, Peng Shu-shen, took me around. He is a spare man of forty-seven, Gary Cooperish in build, who walks with a loose-limbed, swinging rhythm. He started off, unlike any industrial manager I have ever met, by deprecating himself. "I'm a carpenter by trade," he said, "and I've had only three years of school." It later developed that he had previously been assistant manager of the refinery at Taching for eight years, and before that manager of a lumber mill in Tientsin for eleven years. He was able to describe the workings of the computer, and he said that production would be higher with a better computer. He spoke easily of the impact of the Cultural Revolution at the plant. "We didn't have much factionalism here. We started work here only in 1968, and by that time the Cultural Revolution was almost over. We had so much to do that there wasn't much time for factional fights. In fact, we had some students who came to work for us after being trained at the university in Shanghai. I was told that they started off very angry with one another, but that by the time they got here, they had settled half their differences."

I asked him a little about his family. He said, "I have five children. The two oldest are in the army. The others are in school. My wife is a housewife." He makes about $55 per month—a little more than twice the average of an ordinary worker. He has access to a car that belongs to the plant. He said, "I watch the television often in the evening."

At my request, Mr. Peng whistled up the military man who serves on the revolutionary committee that runs the plant—one Chu Wen-chun, a forty-four-year-old soldier, who told me he had the rank of lieutenant colonel. My information was that in many plants the military ran the show, but that was certainly not the case at Peking General Petrochemical. When Colonel Chu showed some hesitation in telling me what kinds

of decisions he had to make on the revolutionary committee, Mr. Peng jumped right in. He cited the case of
a decision on output for the previous month. The state
had asked for 300,000 tons of oil products. That quota
was discussed by the revolutionary committee at the
plant. Some members felt a target higher than 300,000
could be met. But in the end, the decision was to go
for the 300,000 tons. Colonel Chu assured me he had
not made that decision. I came away with the strong
feeling that Mr. Peng had.

I also came away with the strong feeling that heavy
industry in China has a curious, almost unreal quality.
Its workers show none of the disciplined intensity so
familiar in Japan. Its plants do not strain for targets in
the Russian fashion. Its managers conspicuously lack
the king-sized egos of the American executive. It is a
low-pressure system, seemingly disconnected from
the urgent need of agriculture for tractors and fertilizers, and the nascent demand for consumer goods. Part
of the reason, no doubt, is that the central authorities
probably don't have the means to enforce heavy de-
mands. For the time being, the Chinese leaders seem
to have their hands full with larger problems, closer
to home. They are too involved in sorting out the issue
of who rules and what the right set of relations should
be with Russia and the United States to give much
attention to production quotas. The more so as the
chain of command is, to put it mildly, imperfect. Even
officials with some local responsibility seem unsure of
who does what in the capital. When I was visiting the

General Petrochemical plant outside Peking, I asked Colonel Chu of the revolutionary committee a couple of not altogether fair questions to see if he knew that the shake-up of September, 1971, had taken Lin Piao out as defense minister and had also removed Lin's former protégé, Huang Yung-sheng, as army chief of staff. One question was to name the current defense minister. The colonel mentioned Marshal Yeh Chien-ying. The second question was to name the current chief of staff. The colonel first named Wang Tung-hsing, a general known in the past as head of Mao's personal bodyguard. Later I was told that he had made a mistake and that he really meant Wang Hsin-ting, another general now formally listed as vice-chief of staff.

The leadership question, moreover, is entangled with a fundamental question of China's revolutionary mystique. Two good possibilities for rapid expansion of the industrial base exist. China could enter the world market in a big way and acquire through trade —and even more on credit—the know-how, capital, and equipment necessary for mechanization of the countryside. Equally, China could now put decisive emphasis on investment in heavy industry, notably in steel and oil, after the fashion of the United States, Europe, Japan, and the Soviet Union.

The rub there is the Chinese life-style. The ethic of modern China is the ethic of peasant masses. It features the country over the city, work with the hands over work with the head, the simple over the complex, the native over the foreign.

China is about as active in world trade as Mexico. It is still trying to build factories in the countryside. Production of cash crops, as distinct from basic necessities, is stigmatized as "revisionist." Credit is regarded as the instrument of the devil, and serious men have boasted to me that China has no internal or external debt, as if that self-imposed piece of hobbling were a great achievement.

Behind this peasant ethic stands the giant figure of Mao Tse-tung. Support from the countryside brought Mao to the top of the Chinese Communist party. Peasant armies enabled him to take over the country. His historic achievement, as leader and thinker, has been to understand how peasant masses could be recruited for Communism. He is the supreme agrarian radical of world history.

That is why there is now shaping up in China a central clash between the country's needs and its leadership. The absolute requirement of modernizing agriculture can be achieved only after long and chancy travail. It involves the hardest thing in politics—the transition from a heroic leadership to a set of new men. And it raises what is surely the most intriguing question of Chinese life—the question of New Maoist Man.

III

☆

New Maoist Man

A recent Pakistani ambassador to Communist China was startled, when he presented his credentials in Peking not long ago, to receive, instead of the usual diplomatic politesse, a lecture on the nature of man.

A man [the ambassador was told] has only one face, and we can't change that. But we can change what's behind the face. You will see that there is emerging in this country a new kind of man, a Maoist man.

That claim—to be producing a New Maoist Man— is the proudest boast of the Chinese revolution. During the month I passed in China after President Nixon's visit, I found that claim pressed by all kinds of people in all kinds of places at many different times. It was advanced as the rationale for the Cultural Revolution and the Great Leap Forward and most of the other upheavals of the recent past. It was offered as justification for a leadership struggle that continues unabated. It was put forward as the touchstone of what separates the "pure" Communism of Peking from the "revisionist" Communism of Moscow. But is it true? Is a New Maoist Man emerging in Communist China?

That something basic has changed in China is not in doubt. A country once famous for famine has become a groaning board of fish, meat, rice, fruit, and vegetables. The vast inequalities of income that used to separate rich from poor are now compressed in salary scales that give the best-paid managers about only twice the take of the lowliest workers. Class distinctions, made ostentatiously apparent in sedan chairs, palaces, and rich brocades only twenty-five years ago, have been drowned in a sea of bicycles, housing projects, and Mao jackets. Where begging was a way of life, there is now full employment—even for old women, who daily sweep clean formerly filthy streets. Such notorious vices as drug addiction and prostitution have been totally eliminated.

The Chinese themselves show no hesitation in ascribing these changes to personal metamorphosis. At

Tachai, for example, I asked the peasant leader, Chen Yung-kuei, about the origins of his idea for U-shaped retaining walls to support the terraced fields. Chen said, "I noticed that the entrances to our old caves were arc-shaped and never gave way. I also noticed in the towns that bridges supported by arches withstood the floods. So I thought we should arrange the retaining walls in the same shape."

I asked, not without a note of disbelief, how it happened that such a simple idea had never been tried before in the area, where farming had gone on for hundreds, even thousands, of years. Chen said, "I don't know whether they thought about it in the past, but they couldn't have put it into effect if they had. The land was subdivided into many tiny plots, held by many different families. If there had been a suggestion for building retaining walls, everybody would have wanted them built on somebody else's property. Before we could transform the land, we had to transform the people."

The Shanghai editor with whom I had lunched on my first day in China was asked how drug addiction had been abolished. He replied, "Simple. We rounded up all the addicts. We found regular jobs for them. We made them read and study the works of Chairman Mao. After that they were changed persons."

The changed person Chairman Mao seeks to foster is not hard to describe. If it can be said that the French Revolution was directed against the Bourbons, and

the Russian against the czars, then it can also be said
that Mao's revolution aimed to unseat Confucius. Es-
sentially, Maoism poses a philosophic challenge to
China's traditional mandarin ethic with its emphasis
on respect for the powerful, the educated, the rich,
and the old. Mao preaches an egalitarian doctrine that
sanctions strife for the benefit of the whole society. In
his writings, the poor are vaunted over the rich, the
countryside over the city, the uneducated over the
intellectuals, the collective interest over the family or
individual interest, the ruled over the rulers. "Our
customs," Mao once told the French writer André
Malraux, "must become as different from the traditional customs as yours are from feudal customs."

The Maoist mystique is drilled daily into the hearts
and minds of the people of China on a systematic basis
probably unmatched anytime in the past. The Little
Red Books now seem to be out of fashion. But they are
only one tool for indoctrination among many. Soldiers
in their units, workers in their factories, and peasants
in their villages are all assigned regular periods for the
study of the works of Mao. So are students at all levels
from the earliest years to the universities. Hotels in
China carry pamphlets by Mao much as hotels in this
country have the Gideon Bible. Plays, films, and novels all depict heroines and heroes cut in the Maoist
mold. A locally written and produced amateur opera
I saw in Tachai had one whole scene in which a young
girl praised the heroic virtues of a Communist leader

who was shown, silhouetted against the lighted window of his cottage, reading the works of Mao in the lonely watches of the night. In a nursery school I visited in Shanghai, six-year-olds were taught to write by drawing the characters for Mao's slogan "Serve the People." And for those who stray from the straight and narrow there is intensive thought reform in the May 7 schools.

Uniform compliance with the official line finds its most startling expression in the prevailing attitude toward romantic love. I had always supposed that the Chinese were an erotic people. My interpreter confirmed the view that the old practice of foot-binding had sexual implications. "The smaller the feet, the more the suitors was the old saying," he once observed to me. But now sex is repressed with a vengeance. Everybody wears the same basic dress—trousers and tunics, usually in blue or gray. Tunics with polka dots, which I saw occasionally on women in Shanghai and Nanking, were rare enough to command attention. So is the wearing of hair ribbons. It was practically a special event when I saw a soldier holding hands with a waitress in Peking. A twenty-two-year-old bride of a few months whom I met in a village near Peking tittered with embarrassment when I asked her if she and her husband wanted to have children. A young peasant I met in Tachai was positively apologetic when he told me, under questioning, that his wife was eighteen when they married. When I asked an attractive twenty-five-year-old woman worker in Shanghai whether she had a family, she replied, "No. Chairman Mao says we should work and study before marriage. So I'm waiting."

Moreover, the Maoist values have not sunk roots only among the masses. The elites especially are at pains to show their preference for the values of peasant radicalism—for simple ideas over complicated ones, work with the hands over work with the head, for fundamentalist morality, and plainness of style. At a newspaper office in Shanghai I was introduced in the printshop to an editor who was setting type by hand out of a box with four thousand characters. "All our editors do it once a week," I was told. Chi'ao Kuanhua, the deputy foreign minister who negotiated as opposite number to Henry Kissinger during President Nixon's visit, took a month off last year to work with his hands digging a canal near Peking.

One of the most puzzling discussions I had during my entire visit—the most unmeeting of minds—took place with a young woman scientist whom I met in the May 7 school just outside of Peking. She had been detained there for three years—living the hard life of a kind of labor camp, separated from her family, eating plain food and sleeping in a dormitory, working in the fields, and studying the works of Mao. When I met her she was in a study group that had spent three hours discussing an essay by Mao, "On the Source of Correct Ideas." I asked her whether China was so well-endowed with scientists that it could easily afford to keep people of her caliber in the May 7 schools. She said, "We do not have a surplus in this field. The country needs scientists and mathematicians. But I think it is useful to spend time with workers and peasants. It is necessary to rotate jobs in our society."

I said I understood the principle of rotating jobs, but that three years in a May 7 school seemed a little long for rotation. She said, "I have benefited from my stay here. It has remolded my whole world outlook."

I asked her what had been the trouble with her world outlook before. She said, "I was educated at good schools and at the university. I had no contact with working people. For example, I never thought grain was hard to produce. In the past, if I wasted some rice or my children wasted it, I never thought about it. Now I think about it, and I will make my children think about it."

Another person I met in the May 7 school was a middle-aged woman mending on a sewing machine the blue fatigues that serve as a uniform. She came from a middle-class family (her husband was an engineer, as was one of her sons). She had been an amateur painter. "I used to paint in the traditional sense," she said. "Natural scenes, with trees and clouds, sometimes a scholar resting. Now I paint workers and peasants. I think it is better to work here than simply to stay at home. I have come to understand the real purpose of life."

Then there was a thirty-eight-year-old Party worker sent down from Peking. I asked him what he had done that led him to the May 7 school. He said, "I came from a poor family and left school at the age of thirteen after only seven years of education. After 1949, I became a member of the Party, worked in an accounting office, and finally became a Party figure in west Peking. I thought that since my family happened to be workers, I had no need to remold myself at the time of the Cultural Revolution. I was arrogant in my work, and I thought I was marvelous in my person. I thought I was very able, and I looked down on the masses. My general attitude was snobbish.

"When I came here I was confronted with the task of building houses and clearing land. I realized how little I knew. I had to counsel with the peasants, and they taught me. I saw that while I could do nothing by myself, working together we could clear the land and build the houses."

At *Wen Hui Pao*, a main newspaper in Shanghai, I met a reporter who had just finished a series of articles on the management of the government bureau that runs the local shops. I asked him what he had discovered in covering the Commercial Bureau. He said, "The leaders of the Commercial Bureau have recently been reading the works of Karl Marx, especially *Civil War in France*. As a result, they have come much closer to the masses. There was one leader in the bureau who was afraid to go to the people. He just used to sit in his office and do everything by telephone. Now he goes out and visits the shops all the time. He makes decisions that are closer to reality."

A middle-aged apparatchik who took me around Nanking told me this story about his experiences in the Cultural Revolution: "There was a time when I was in school, and even after, when I wanted to earn lots of money. But in the Cultural Revolution I learned this was very selfish. I learned that I ought to serve the people body and soul . . . and not only the people in this province but the people in the world. I discovered in the peasant a higher revolutionary consciousness than I had . . . even on international affairs. One peasant once spoke to me about Vietnam. He said, 'Our brothers there are bleeding, so we can afford to sweat a little. The more we sweat, the less they will bleed!' "

Riding from Nanking to Shanghai on a train, a government official was talking about how much China had changed in the past twenty-five years. He said, "In the past, the usual form of greeting was to ask, 'Have you eaten?' Now there is plenty of food so we don't say that. The usual way to say good-bye was, 'Give my regards to your father.' That was because the father was always dominant in every family. But now that's not true anymore. The authority of the father is questioned every day."

In Tachai, I asked a peasant leader what was the difference between Maoist Man and non-Maoist Man.

He said, "The attitude toward self. There will always be some self. But the difference is whether the self comes first or the public comes first. We think it is good for the public to come first and the self second."

I asked him how many of the peasants in his village shared that view. He said, "About 95 percent of the people. There are some individual exceptions. But not many."

At a small cottage-type transistor plant outside Peking, I met an attractive seventeen-year-old girl who was in charge of about half a dozen people rolling wires for transformers. I asked her how she and other young people felt about the absence of love stories, or indeed any boy-girl stuff, in the eight revolutionary operas. She said, "A love story, of course, is part of the world. But it is a matter of individual feeling. It shouldn't be in an opera, which should express high ideals."

I asked her why individual feelings shouldn't have just as important a place in the operas as high ideals. She said, "Young people need ideals in order to build up the country. As to personal matters, such as love, it is all right to think about them. But they do not have priority. Priority goes to building up the country."

Literature offers perhaps the most dramatic measure of the transformation in elite attitudes. China enjoyed in the first part of this century much the same kind of prerevolutionary renaissance that flowered in Russia before 1917. In particular, there was Lu Hsun, an essayist and writer of short fiction preeminent in Chinese intellectual life, who ranks as a figure of importance even in world literature. He wrote of Dante, Dostoevski, and Don Quixote as well as of the Chinese classics. He met Shaw in Shanghai and took the measure of him in an essay that begins: "George Bernard Shaw is not making a world cruise. He is traveling to see reporters' faces all over the world." He cared about painting as well as writing, and he had trouble in medical school, which he attended in Japan at the turn of the century, because he kept submitting diagrams of the arm that showed the veins and arteries placed more in keeping with his aesthetic sense than the anatomical facts.

For the last fifteen years of his life, Lu Hsun worked with the Communists, and he is now their chief literary hero. There is a Lu Hsun museum in Shanghai, and his home there is preserved as a shrine. One of the early clues to the disappearance of Lin Piao, the former defense minister and heir apparent to Mao Tsetung, was an article in the *People's Daily* of September 25, 1971, marking the ninetieth anniversary of Lu Hsun's birth, which cited a critique he had made of Confucius. The critique, which apparently spelled out to the cognoscenti in China the behavior that brought Lin Piao to grief, was that "Confucius made colorful plans to govern the country; however, all his plans were for those who govern the people and for those in power. He did not make any plans for the people themselves. Therefore . . . he was nothing but a 'sage' of those in power or those who wished to be in power, and had nothing to do with the people at large."

Lu Hsun's specialty was the *tsa wen*, or dagger, a short, sharply pointed satirical piece, and he did not spare even the Communists. "Though all literature is propaganda," he wrote toward the end of his life, in a dig at the Party, "not all propaganda is literature." Even when first agreeing to work for the revolution, his doubts came to the surface:

> Imagine an iron house without windows [he wrote], absolutely indestructible, with many people inside who will soon die of suffocation. But you know since they will die in their sleep, they will not feel any of the pain of death. Now if you cry aloud to wake a few of the lighter sleepers, making those unfortunate few suffer the agony of irrevocable death, do you think you are going to do them a good turn?

Lu Hsun died in 1936, but writers associated with him, and sharing some of his genius, continued the tradition of working with the Party while directing *tsa wen* against it. The woman novelist Ting Ling was the editor of a Party paper and the author of a novel, *The Sun Shines Over the Sangkan River*, which won a Stalin Prize in the early 1950s. But in one of her short stories, a character complains that "we teachers have to be guided by the so-called commissioners of popular education," and in a speech in 1953, she told a writers' congress that "to write a good book should be our objective." The poet Ai Ching joined the Communists in Yenan, but even in that paradise of self-sacrifice complained in a well-known essay that the writer cannot be "a Mongolian lark which never sings anything but praises." The novelists Mao Tun and Lao She and the belletrist Kuo Mo-jo also worked for the Party and against some of its hard-line orthodoxy. Most of them were silenced in the harsh crackdown that followed the Let a Hundred Flowers Bloom period of 1956–57, but even after that writers of strong, independent views and undoubted sophistication continued to work inside Communist China. In 1961 and 1962, the fight against Chairman Mao by the Party leadership under Liu Shao-ch'i was waged through the agency of at least two writers of high talent. Wu Han, a historian and deputy mayor of Peking, wrote a play and series of essays on Hai Jui, an official in the Ming dynasty, who warns the emperor against harsh treatment of his subjects. In one bold sally against Chairman Mao, Wu Han has Hai Jui tell the emperor: "In earlier years you did a few good things, but . . . all officials in and out of the capital know that your mind is not right, that you are too arbitrary, too perverse. You think you alone are right, you refuse to accept criticism and your mistakes are many. . . ."

Teng T'o, a former editor of the *People's Daily* and

Party ideologist in Peking, made slashing attacks on Mao in a collection of essays that bears the title *Evening Talks at Yenshan*. In one essay entitled "Big Talk," Teng T'o put into the mouth of a child a rare burlesque of the Maoist style and the slogan about the East wind prevailing over the West wind. "There is in my neighborhood," Teng T'o wrote, "a child who has recently often imitated the ring of a great poet and composed quite a number of 'big talks.' Not long ago he wrote a piece called 'Ode to the Wild Grass,' which rang with empty talk. He wrote:

> The sky is our father,
> The earth our mother,
> The sun our nurse,
> The East wind our benefactor,
> The West wind our enemy."

The first shots of the cultural revolution picked off Wu Han and Teng T'o, and subsequent salvos practically obliterated literature itself. So far as I can determine no new books, apart from the Little Red Book of Chairman Mao's dicta, were published at all between 1966 and 1970. Literature, the stage, films, ballet, and music were dominated by the eight model revolutionary operas staged and shaped by Chiang Ch'ing, or Madame Mao, from texts written years before. Seven of the eight pieces—*Red Detachment of Women, Taking*

*Tiger Mountain by Strategy, The White-Haired Girl,
Shajiabang, The Red Latern, The Yellow River Concerto,*
and *Raid on the White Tiger Regiment*—are set in the
period of the patriotic war against Japan and the civil
war against Chiang Kai-shek and the Kuomintang. In
all of them, Communist heroes engage and subdue
double-dyed villains: the leading Kuomintang man in
Taking Tiger Mountain, for instance, is called Vulture
and his men are called the Terribles. Friendly relations exist between only mothers and sons, fathers and
daughters, uncles and nephews, or the old and the
very young. There is no romance, no scene even between husband and wife, and there were protests recently when a visiting Japanese troupe playing *The
White-Haired Girl* had a young man bestow upon a girl
a piece of red ribbon that was, in the original, given
by her father. The dance features women stretching
heavenward in torment and anguish, men in stances
of decision, heads firm and eyes blazing. The arias,
played to music that seems to fuse Wagner and Sousa,
are patriotic declamations. "Not one inch of our fair
land will we surrender," goes one from *Shajiabang,*
"nor will we tolerate the brutality of the Japanese
invader." Here is a bit of dialogue from the same play:

> LING: Young Wang! Come and let me change
> your dressing.
> WANG: Change the dressing? No I won't.
> LING: Why not?

WANG: Little Ling, it's so hard to get medicine.
We should keep it for serious cases.

Since the disappearance of Lin Piao, there has been
an undoubted change in the cultural atmosphere.
During my visit, the Little Red Book of Chairman
Mao was not available at Chinese bookstores—perhaps because it had a preface by Lin Piao, but more
likely because it is being deemphasized in general. I
was told by one knowledgeable foreign diplomat to
buy, as an item that was vanishing never to be produced again, an alarm that rang when a Little Red
Book emerged from the clockwork to strike a bell. A
new opera, *Ode to Dragon River*, which also seems to
have some implications for the Lin Piao affair, was
reprinted in full by literary reviews in Shanghai and
Peking. It tells the story of a woman, Chian Sui-ying,
who is the Party secretary of a village near the river.
Access to water enables the village to enjoy a fine year
at the very time other villages are experiencing
drought. Miss Chian perceives that water can be
brought to the other villages across the fields of her
own village. Since that involves the risk of flooding,
the peasants in her village protest. She prevails, however, and her village is temporarily flooded. In the end,
the other villages are saved and her village also has a
good crop.

One of the literary papers that reprinted *Ode to
Dragon River* was *Kuang Ming*, or Clarity, a daily pub-

lished in Peking with about 120,000 circulation. I
visited *Kuang Ming* and talked about operas, old and
new, with the editor, Chang Ch'ang-hai, a highly ar-
ticulate literary gentleman in his fifties. He said that
Ode to Dragon River was based on events that actually
took place in Fukien Province, and that the story was
a group production, written by several writers based
in Shanghai. I asked him why he felt it merited re-
printing in its entirety. He said, "The important thing
about *Ode to Dragon River* is that it takes place under
the Red flag. In other operas, the conflict is between
ourselves and our enemies. Here the conflict is among
ourselves, among those who have backward ideas and
those who have advanced ideas. The tension is between Communists with narrow views and Communists with larger views. The purpose of the opera is to
educate comrades to the larger view. You see, very few
people would openly advocate selfish behavior. They
would not say 'let us prevent those drought-ridden
villages from getting water.' But they would say 'let us
avoid flooding our fields.' This opera shows how un-
duly small collective views can be quite selfish."

I also asked why the older operas had no scenes
between man and wife, no love interest. He said,
"There are always bound to be personal sentiments—
love between husband and wife. Naturally we do not
deny the facts of life in our society. But this is a question of the education of the people, and on that point
Chairman Mao spoke clearly many years ago. It is

more important to show class relations than to show personal relations. The broad masses want something more lofty than personal relations. They do not want to concentrate, and it is not our purpose to have them concentrate, on so-called love. We want them to think about the millions of oppressed people. The lofty thing in literature is to show oppression."

I asked for an example of a young writer who showed oppression, and was given the name of Hao Jan, the author of a trilogy, *The Sun Shines Bright*, which had been published between 1964 and 1966, and was now being republished. The Information Department of the Foreign Office, which guided my tour, arranged for me to meet him, and we got together in Peking at the International Club. It was a droll choice, dictated, I suppose, by the absence of cafés or bars or other places to meet in Peking. Except for a brown board at the entrance with freshly gilded letters announcing Members Notices, the International Club is in every particular a classic case of vanished splendor —a virtually unused white, wooden structure with peeling paint, landscaping gone to seed, an empty swimming pool, and a volleyball court where tennis used to be played. About Hao Jan, however, there is nothing faded. He is a vigorous forty, with the broad nose and crew cut of a peasant; only the pen he carried in his breast pocket suggested a writer. He bounced up from his chair when I came into the club, spouted greetings, and never seemed to stop talking thereafter.

"The literary and art world of China," he said, "consists of two kinds of people. There are the old intellectuals and there are the people who came forth during the war and the construction period. The latter are more vigorous. Indeed, the former are not vigorous at all, partially because of age and partially because they have yet to become acclimated to the new situation. I belong to the latter group. I was the son of a peasant. It was at the end of the War of Liberation against Japan that I became a writer. I was born in 1932. I had three years in primary school. In 1946, aged fourteen, I joined the revolutionary forces. I was in the base area in Chi County, in Hopei Province, one hundred miles from Peking. Very few people there had any education. Since I had primary school, they let me write propaganda in verse. Never previously did a peasant's son take up the pen. So at first I was nervous. I started by writing small snatches for the operas and even playing some parts. I also made up verses for wall posters. Later on I wrote for newspapers. From 1949 to 1954, I combined work with study. I became obsessed with literature. I truly came to love it. In 1954 I went to work for the paper in Hopei Province, reporting on peasant activities and gathering material for a book. In 1958 I published a collection of short stories. It was my first book—*The Magpie on the Twig.*With the publication of that book, I finally realized my dream to become a writer. Ever since I have never laid down my pen. I have worked steadily and

I love it. I have published seventeen books. *The Sun Shines Bright* had a million three hundred thousand words. It sold a million copies. The booksellers told me that if we had published five million copies, we would now have sold five million copies."

I asked Hao about his recent work. He said, "I work from eight to twelve in the morning and from two to four in the afternoon. I live in the countryside, and evenings I visit the peasants and have heart-to-heart talks with them. Sometimes I spend whole days working with them in the fields. Right now I'm working on a full-length novel which I hope to publish on the thirtieth anniversary of the speech on literature and art that Chairman Mao gave in Yenan. It is the story of how the Chinese peasant became collectivized. As you know, Chinese agriculture has been backward for almost two thousand years. After land was distributed to the peasant in the reform of 1949, it was not easy to switch from individual farming to collective farming. The peasants had to change not only ownership, they also had to change their thinking. The idea that prevailed is the idea that this is mine, that is yours. The distinction was very sharp. The rich peasants played on that idea to try to disrupt the transition. The aim of the novel is to portray the complexity of the transition. The story shows how Socialism serves the poor peasants. It shows how if it were undone, everything would come apart."

I asked Hao Jan whether he didn't have troubles

during the Cultural Revolution and previous periods of difficulty for writers. He said, "Since I took up the pen I've had some stormy days. First I was unsure of myself and did not dare write. After I was published and enjoyed some fame, I became very self-satisfied. I compared myself with some of the older writers, and I thought, 'I produce more than they do but they have a more comfortable life than I do.' They tried to tempt me. They wanted me to divorce myself from the peasants. For a while they nearly succeeded. I almost thought my aim in life was to reach their status—to write about historical subjects. But I went down to the countryside for a few years, and I came to see the truth. I came to see my own faults. I came to understand that literature and art should be only a spare part in the machinery of revolution."

My exchanges with Hao Jan were conducted through the translator who had been assigned to me by the Foreign Office and who went wherever I did. He was very nice personally, and highly skilled, but he also had a certain obvious standing in official quarters. It occurred to me that some of the lines I was hearing—lines like literature being a "spare part of the revolution," which was straight out of Lenin as cited by Mao—were put-ons, mouthed less for my ears than for those of my translator. So I asked to have at least one meeting entirely alone, and without a translator. It happened—either by quirk of circumstance or because my suspicions were unfounded or because the

Chinese are just plain clever—that the man I was allowed to see alone would have been last on my list of those offered by the Chinese for a solo interview. He was Chien Wei-chang, a well-known physicist, trained at the Jet Propulsion Laboratory at the California Institute of Technology, who reputedly plays an important role in the Chinese nuclear program.

I had first met Dr. Chien when I visited Tsinghua University, the leading technical school in Peking, where he is a professor and vice-chairman of the revolutionary committee. He was one of a group of professors and students who had been assembled to meet me. I had been told at Tsinghua that during the Cultural Revolution the institution had been transformed from an elite academy into a school for the people. There had been twelve thousand students, all newly graduated from the best middle schools in China. "They were," one professor said, "three-door cadres—they went from the door of the home to the door of the university to the door of a government office." Between 1965 and 1971, students in the six-year course had been allowed to graduate, but no new students were admitted. In 1972, the university began from scratch, with students chosen from the ranks of the army, the factories, or the agricultural communes. The basis of choice was ideological rather than academic; there were discussions, not examinations; and students, far from being obliged to listen to their professors, were allowed to talk at any time.

I tried to probe these claims with—perhaps because my approach was too brusque—little success. I asked a professor of political science what he was teaching his students about the role of Lin Piao in the Cultural Revolution and his sudden disappearance. The professor said, "I have no comment to make on that." A student jumped in and said to me, "You have no right to ask that question."

I raised with a girl student who had come to the university from a state farm the issue of whether all the people in the countryside didn't want to come to the city. I even asked her, at one point, "How ya gonna keep 'em down on the farm after they've seen Peking?" She did not understand the question and did not make any reply. But one of her professors said, "I understand why you ask that question because that's what I used to think. Life in the city is more comfortable than life in the country. Before the Cultural Revolution, I used to think of myself and my comfort. We even used to have a saying at the university about students who came from the country: 'In the first year they lead simple lives; in the second year, they forget about the simple life; in the third year, they don't recognize their parents.' But that's not what the workers or peasants are thinking. We ask ourselves what is more important, personal comfort or to raise the standard of living of the 80 or 90 percent of the Chinese people who live in the countryside."

Another professor said, "There are two ways to do

things. There are people who plant what others eat, and there are people who eat what others plant. We prefer the first. You prefer the second."

I tried to get at the role of the army on campus, particularly when it came to settling scores between the various factions that had formed in the student body during the Cultural Revolution. My impression was that there had been something like pitched battles between troops and students at Tsinghua. But one student told me, "The military men came to the university at a time when we were still fighting among ourselves. But they did not act as referees or umpires or say who was right and who was wrong. They opened study classes so we could discover for ourselves what was right and what was wrong. They had heart-to-heart talks with us."

I asked to see one of the army officers serving on the revolutionary committee that runs the university. He appeared, but refused to answer any questions about his rank or unit. When I asked him what he was doing at the university, he repeated a phrase from Mao: "My job is to support the Left." When I asked him what he meant, he said, "Perhaps your understanding of the so-called Left and the so-called Right is different from ours."

At that point I called it quits. Before leaving, I asked if I could visit the home of a professor. Professor Chien, a mild, soft-spoken, white-haired man, who had been relatively silent and certainly not hostile, said I could come to his place. It turned out to be a charming home—bedroom, study, living room, and kitchen—arranged around a small courtyard. There were books everywhere, in English, Russian, and German, as well as Chinese. Most of the material was technical—I noted the *Theory of Atomic Collisions* by Mott and Massey and a complete set of the *Journal of Applied Mathematics and Mechanics*. There was also a set of Lu Hsun's works. On the walls were pictures of the heroes in the operas *Shajiabang* and *The Red Lantern*. There was also a print of a well-known painting— *Spring Rain on Li River*—by Hsu Bei-won, an artist who had worked with the French Impressionists. We talked a little in English about how hard it was to keep up in physics and mathematics. It developed that Professor Chien had known in his California days some physicists, including Robert Oppenheimer, whom I had known when I was at the Institute for Advanced Study at Princeton. I asked him if we could get together for dinner. He seemed willing, so I extended a formal invitation through the Foreign Office. The invitation was accepted, and the Foreign Office also, to my surprise, accepted my stipulation that since it was my dinner, we wouldn't need the translator.

The dinner took place in a private room in the Minzu restaurant, which I figured to be a neutral place since the cuisine was Mongol and I had first been taken there by a Russian diplomat. I had been able to order in advance, so we had a chance for steady talk.

I started by mentioning the difference between Lu Hsun, who seemed to me so original, and the best-selling novelist Hao Jan, whom I had seen earlier that day. Professor Chien said, "Lu Hsun was living at a time of great turmoil and revolutionary consciousness. There were the hard times of the 1930s, the war against Japan, the imperialist presence in Shanghai, and the issue of whether China should follow a Socialist road or a capitalist road. All that was unsettled."

"You make it sound," I said, "as though it were easier to be a great writer at that time than now."

He said, "Of course. It was much easier in the bitter times of the 1930s to be a good Communist, a good revolutionary, a good anything. Now we have to keep educating our young people all the time. Otherwise they will slip backward. The purpose of the Cultural Revolution was to create the atmosphere of the 1930s for our young people. Now they know what a struggle is."

He then proceeded indirectly but unmistakably to criticize me for posing questions about Lin Piao and other figures in the leadership. "I have heard," he said, "that you keep asking who did what, and what happened to whom. I must tell you that you will never learn anything by such questions. Who's Who counts for nothing in China. You have to ask which is the right road, which is the wrong road. That way you will learn. We are used to twenty years of changes. We don't pay much attention to who is up and who is down. Those kinds of changes are not important."

I replied that I had difficulty taking seriously the notion of the right road and the wrong road, and even the whole formula that "one divides into two." I pointed out that in the United States, we usually had a wide variety of choices in any particular situation. "In my country," I said, "one often divides into nineteen or thirty-four or forty-seven or more."

He said that the formula "one divides into two" represented the class interest. In every situation, there was the interest of those who ruled and of those who were ruled. I objected that I didn't really see the class side of it—even in China. It seemed to me that when the Chinese spoke now of landlords and rich peasants it was as though they were speaking of dragons. In fact, the landlords and rich peasants didn't exist anymore and couldn't have any real influence.

He explained that it was mainly a matter of attitude, that all people had inside themselves thoughts and emotions that were part of the outlook of the ruling class. "I myself have those thoughts and emotions sometimes," he said. "So do you." I insisted that I really didn't think that such an analysis was useful. I asked him who he thought ruled the United States.

"The monopolists," he said flatly.

I told him that in my view the United States was not run by the monopolists. I said, "If any single group runs the United States, it is the lower middle class. They have the majority. They dominate all the elections."

He said, "Well, we could debate that for a long time.

But we can't settle it this evening, and we have only this evening to talk."

I asked him about China's work in space, observing that the Chinese had put up a satellite. "No," he corrected me, "we have two satellites. But they are only for scientific purposes."

I asked him if he found the satellites that useful scientifically. I said that some American scientists had doubts about the value of our space program and felt that it was undertaken mainly for prestige reasons.

He acknowledged the prestige element in the space program. As far as the Chinese program goes, he said, "we have found that two satellites are enough."

I mentioned to him a phrase that I could not understand that the Chinese kept using all through the President's visit. That was the phrase "The American people are a great people, and the Chinese people are a great people." I said it didn't seem very meaningful to me because the Chinese also said the Russians were a great people. "Would you," I asked, "also say that the Japanese are a great people?"

He said, "Yes, the Japanese are a great people."

"But if you say everybody is a great people," I put in, "then it doesn't have any meaning. Then it's an empty phrase, like 'the East is Red.' "

He ignored that little thrust but said with great seriousness, "If you think about China and what we have thought about ourselves in the past, I think you will understand that it is very meaningful for us to say that we are not greater than you are. It is important for China to say that we are not greater than any other people. That is a fundamental principle."

I observed that another aspect of the Chinese approach that I didn't understand well was the business about fundamental principles. I said, "You always insist on settling principles first. We believe in principles in the United States, but we think they are something you carry around in the back of the head, not talking about them too much. We think that, in the interests of practical achievement, it is sometimes a good idea not to let abstract ideas get in the way. We believe in settling principles last."

He said, "That is the great difference between us. When you aren't clear about principles, then you always have an endless number of petty arguments about details. That is why one doesn't divide into two for you. That is why you think that one divides into nineteen or thirty-four or forty-seven or more."

As we prepared to leave, I asked the restaurant to call me a cab. I offered him a lift. He smiled and shook his head. He pointed to a large brown car that was clearly an official vehicle. He said, "No, I don't need a lift. I have my car."

It wasn't, of course, his car; no individual in China owns an auto. This one belonged to the university and had been made available to Dr. Chien for the evening. Still, the phrase "my car" was eloquent of a prevailing attitude, a carry-over from the bad old days that goes against the central precept of New Maoist Man. Despite the claims for equality achieved through a steady turning of the revolutionary wheel, the interest in worldly goods, and with it the distinction in status, has not died in China. Most of the top Communist leaders travel in large cars. Marshal Yeh Chien-ying, who seems to be the leading military official now, has a Mercedes. The one Jaguar I saw in Peking belongs to a police unit. The editor of *Wen Hui Pao*, the newspaper I visited in Shanghai, has the top-floor corner office and three phones on his desk. Though officer ranks have technically been eliminated, the military man I met at the Peking petrochemical plant told me that he had the rank of lieutenant colonel. Riding on a sleeper, I saw another military man and was assured that he was an officer. I asked how his rank was known. "He wouldn't be traveling on a sleeper," I was told, "if he wasn't an officer."

Hao Jan, the novelist, acknowledged to me that, among other things, he had bought three bicycles with his royalties. The head of a commune, or village, outside Nanking proudly informed me that last year's crop had been so good the commune had been able to buy a television set; three more were on order. A very earnest Party official in Nanking, who at one point apologized because there were still pedicabs impelled by human labor, also gave me the following account of his family life.

I work and my wife works. Our five-year-old goes to school. Our two-year-old is left at home. But there is an old lady in the neighborhood. She comes to stay with the child and clean the flat in the daytime. We do not pay her. But we take her to the movies on Sunday and things like that. She is very glad to help us. Often she says to me, "Usually at my age it is the end. But for me it is the beginning. I am helping you to build Socialism."

People who find such an ingenious way to explain having what Europeans call a servant and Americans know as help cannot be expected to swallow whole the Maoist strictures against traditional family life. I met dozens of middle-aged persons who had parents living with them. Repeatedly I found cases of young working couples who had sent their children to live with grandparents. Chinese I encountered traveling were almost always going to visit relatives. I asked one old man who I met in a remote village whether any of his children wanted to visit Peking. He said, "Why should they want to visit Peking? They don't have any relatives there."

Despite the claimed waning of parental authority, moreover, the Communists themselves constantly cite the examples of the fathers to influence the behavior of the sons. One of the scenes in the village opera I saw at Tachai, for example, shows a young man who is splitting rocks with a mace as part of a program for building stone houses. At one point, after being ridiculed by a rich peasant, the boy approaches the local Party leader and laments that he has terrible blisters on his hands and that he really isn't getting anywhere cracking the rocks. The Party leader then tells the young man a story about a mason who worked for a cruel landlord in the old days before the Communist take-over. The landlord, at one point, refused to pay the mason for some work he had done, and the mason starved to death. Just before he died, the mason confined his only son to the care of the local Party man. At that point, the young man with the blisters says to the local Party functionary, "Don't give me another story about the old days."

But the Party man continues. It develops that the mason was none other than the father of the young man with the blisters, who was, in fact, brought up by the father of the local Party secretary. "If your father could see you now," the Party man says to the complaining youngster, "he would be ashamed. He would say, 'How can you be afraid of the difficulties for which I died.'" At that point in the opera, the complaining youngster melts in the arms of the Party official. "Oh, Uncle," he says, using a term of respect, "It is as if I woke from a dream. I will never forget how my father died. Give me the hardest work there is. I will undertake my best to sustain all my tasks and to build our country and Socialism."

Similar use of parental influence is made in the trilogy *The Sun Shines Bright* by Hao Jan. The drama turns on a young man who is drawn by a rich peasant to work against the Communist leader of the village. The young man's father brings the boy back to the straight and narrow. At one point, the father says to the son, "We were poor people. We must follow the Party all our lives and never change heart." And the novelist comments, "This was a father's call to his son. . . ."

At another point, the author describes the son's reaction to the father's pressure in this way: "He saw clearly what his father expected him to do, and he realized that his father's challenge was correct and that he should take it up. Everyone should do his best to fulfill such a request as his father had made—a request not to be denied."

If the claims for New Maoist Man are unsaid directly by surviving instincts for family life and worldly goods, they are probably more severely weakened by an indirect, subversive challenge. The Confucian tradition combines with the peasant instinct for ducking under the waves of history, to breed in China a deep capacity for temporary adjustment—for conforming superficially without believing deep down, for paying lip service to official truths. I found an example even in that arcanum of Maoist orthodoxy, the commune of Tachai. Visiting the village school, I asked children in several classrooms where they wanted to live after graduation. Most said they wanted to stay in the village. A few did not reply—a muteness I put down to shyness or uncertainty. But several hours later, the official who had taken me around the village observed, "There are still young people here who want to go to the cities." I asked him how he knew. He said, "From those who didn't respond when you asked them where they wanted to live."

Elsewhere in China I repeatedly encountered wry and ironic remarks, sly witticisms, and deliberate bits of absurdity all pointing to skepticism regarding elements of the Maoist mystique. Dr. Chien, the physicist from Tsinghua, spent a considerable time telling me about what he called the "lure of the countryside" on his students. In time, the discussion came round to young scientists. He said that China had developed a number of very good young scientists even in the highly theoretical field of small-particle physics. Half facetiously, I asked him if the brilliant young physicists were very susceptible to the "lure of the countryside." He said, "A lot of good things grow in the countryside. But not physicists."

At one middle school I visited, the students were reading the *Anti-Dühring*, an essay written by Marx's partner, Friedrich Engels, in a rejoinder to an attack on Marxism by the Berlin philosopher Eugen Dühring. I expressed some surprise to the teacher that Chinese students could really be interested in such an obscure piece of European intellectual history. I then began going round the room asking the students to identify Dühring. None of them could. When I turned to the teacher and said that proved there was little interest, he said, "Well, we're only reading excerpts."

At the May 7 school, I came across a group that had been reading *The Communist Manifesto*. In response to my question, someone recited the opening sentence: "A spectre is haunting Europe. The spectre of Communism." I observed that the spectre of Communism did not really haunt Europe anymore—that France and West Germany and Britain and Scandinavia, in particular, were a long way from yielding to Communist subversion or penetration. One member of the study group said, "You have to remember that *The Communist Manifesto* was written in 1848. Marxism-Leninism has improved since then."

At the office of the newspaper *Kuang Ming* in Peking, I asked one of the editors why the paper hadn't carried at least some report of a story I had broken about a meeting of Premier Chou En-lai with the leaders of North Vietnam just after President Nixon's China visit. The editor said, "We saw the story, and we know that often foreign journalists have accurate information about our leaders before we do. But we also know that foreign journalists are sometimes wrong. So we didn't print the story."

I asked if they had made an effort to check on the story with the Foreign Ministry or anybody else. "No," was the answer, and then the editor, brightening, said, "But if you find out anything more, I wish you'd let us know."

In the end, I suppose, the question I have posed respecting New Maoist Man has to be given a double answer. To a remarkable degree, the Chinese accept and observe the Maoist teachings. They do so in a disciplined fashion, obviously responsive to the pressure of the leadership. But that conformity must not be dismissed purely as a tactically smart response to Communist authority. Such disciplined conformity, for one thing, does not exist everywhere in the Communist world; it does not exist in the Soviet Union. Moreover, many things learned by rote, and mouthed out of calculation, become in time the substance of true belief. To a large extent that seems to have happened in China. As the ambassador who was told on presenting his credentials that he was going to see a New Maoist Man said, "Maoism is a kind of religion."

Still, the Chinese believers are not old-time true believers. Fanatical devotion is curbed by the levity and skepticism of a cultivated people. I never saw a Chinese official strain, as Russian officials so often strain, to put a blatant act of self-interest within the ambit of the official line. Neither did I ever see a Chinese, after the fashion of so many Americans, show unease because behavior was not up to the standards of the ruling ethic. The Chinese know that their belief is a belief. They are supreme actors, mindful that somewhere there is a line between what is theater and what is real, what is art and what is life. That self-consciousness, that ability to be pragmatic about belief, to use a religion, is what sets the Chinese apart from everybody else. It is the Chinese difference.

Premier Chou En-lai, the most notable flesh-and-blood exemplar of the Chinese difference, made the point himself at a private dinner he gave for the President and his staff after the visit to the Great Wall. In his toast the premier cited a poem by Mao written around the Chinese proverb that "to see the Wall is to become a man." The tone seemed lukewarm, and afterward one of the Americans said to Chou, "Mr. Prime Minister, you give me the impression you're not really sure that we went to the Great Wall today."

Chou replied, "You have a very Chinese mind."